How to Build the
GRANDMA
CONNECTION

THE COMPLETE POCKET GUIDE

How to Build the
GRANDMA
CONNECTION

Susan V. Bosak, MA

TCP PRESS
TORONTO

Published by
TCP Press
9 Lobraico Lane
Whitchurch-Stouffville, Ontario
L4A 7X5 Canada
(905) 640-8914   www.tcppress.com

Visit www.grandmaconnection.org for updates, tips, and more

Publishing Coordination: Brian A. Puppa
Design and Production: Douglas A. Bosak
Printing and Binding: Webcom

This book is bound using Otabind – Webcom's exclusive, durable
binding process. The book lays flat and the spine, which is separated
from the binding, remains crisp and new.

ATTENTION SCHOOLS, SERVICE ORGANIZATIONS, AND BUSINESSES:
Quantity discounts are available for educational, business, or promo-
tional use for *How to Build the Grandma Connection* and *Something to
Remember Me By*. Call TCP Press at 1-800-772-7765.

Canadian Cataloguing in Publication Data

Bosak, Susan V.
   How to build the grandma connection : the complete pocket guide

Includes bibliographical references and index.
ISBN 1-896232-03-5

1. Grandparenting.   2. Grandparent and child.   I. Title.

HQ759.9.B67 2000   306.874'5   C00-930672-2

Printed and bound in Canada
09 08 07 06 05 04   10 9 8 7 6 5 4 3

For a grandmother from the past,
my "Baba" Eva Krawchuk,
and for two grandmothers in the present,
Erin Zimmer and Margaret Puppa.
Each built a loving grandma connection
in their own special way.

Contents

*"Each time of life
has its own kind of love."*

Leo Tolstoy, *Family Happiness*

Introduction:
If You Build It,
They Will Come

THE BOY MIGHT HAVE BEEN seven or eight years old. He stood in line with his grandmother at a book signing after a talk I'd done for grandparents and grandchildren. As he inched closer, you could see this little guy had something on his mind. I would glance up at him every once in a while between signing books. He was almost bursting! Finally, it was his turn. He handed me a book to sign. "You know what?" he started. I listened expectantly. "My grandma can beat up your grandma!" I wasn't quite sure what to say. "Oh?" I responded with surprise. "Yeah, she's great!" he concluded with a big grin. An embarrassed grandma then quickly explained that she had recently helped her grandson deal with a bully – nonviolently, of course!

Children may express it in different ways, but I've seen how much they love their grandparents. They need and want a close connection. If you work at building the grandparent connection, what you give will be returned tenfold.

I know firsthand that many grandparents are just as eager as their grandchildren to have a close connection. Thousands of people have come to my Grandma Connection Workshops to learn how to navigate the often challenging, modern territory of grandparenthood and build closer bonds with their grandchildren and adult children.

Perhaps you're just moving into the "grand generation." Many baby boomers are heading into this part of their lives. You might be worried that this is synonymous with getting "old." Not so! People today are living longer, healthier lives. And research shows one of the keys to aging well is being involved in meaningful activity. Active grandparenting can be very meaningful. The definition of "grand" is:

magnificent; splendid; noble; wonderful or very pleasing; of great importance and distinction

Grandparenting can offer the joys and benefits of parenting, without the hassles, constraints, and day-to-day responsibilities.

This doesn't mean, though, that you can take being a grandparent for granted. It isn't always an easy or straightforward relationship. Relationships today can be complicated by busy schedules, working parents and grandparents, divorce, and distance. Even under the best circumstances, grandparenting does not necessarily come naturally – certainly no more naturally than good parenting. Like any human relationship, being a grandparent is something you have to work at and work through. Some research indicates that despite their best intentions or hopes, only 20% of grandparents actually have a very close connection with their grandchildren. Grandparents can fool themselves into believing otherwise – they want it to be different – but the reality is that they don't really know their grandchildren, nor do they put enough time into building a close bond.

When an article on my work appeared in *The Washington Post*, over 3,000 calls poured in. Many were from new grandparents wanting to learn more about how to build a close, lifelong relationship with their grandchildren. More interesting was that many calls were from young mothers wondering how to get grandparents more involved in their children's lives. Grandparent or parent, the desire is there. But, particularly with so many changes in the family, we don't seem to be quite sure how to actually build the all-important grandparent connection. There's no magic. I've found that most people just need to be reminded what it's all about, and then use some simple guidelines to put all the pieces together in a way that works for them.

I use my book *Something to Remember Me By* as the starting point in my workshops. It captures the essence of the grandparent connection. When I share the story with grandparents and parents, they immediately "get it." My grandmother inspired the book. I was very close to her from the time I was a little girl.

There's a line that's repeated in *Something to Remember Me By*: "She gave her a big, warm smile and a warm, snuggly hug." That's it, right there, in one sentence. That's the timeless essence of the grandparent connection. That's what we all need – whether you're a child or a grown-up. Most of the time I think it's just that simple. That's why I think that *Something to Remember Me By*, a simple, little, 32-page children's picture book, has become a best-selling gift book. This story about a little girl and her grandmother and their special relationship over the years is a way to say "I love you" to your grandchild. But adults have this amazing emotional reaction to it, too. People give it to their mothers and grandmothers because it gets to the heart of something we need – and perhaps we feel like we're missing.

A grandmother in Florida wrote to me to say that she spotted *Something to Remember Me By* in her bookstore, began reading it – and started crying right where she stood. She took a seat, read the book through, and cried some more. She said the story reminded her of her grandma. But she was also thinking about her two little granddaughters, who are eighteen months and three years, and live far away from her. She said that right there in the bookstore, she made a promise to herself to do everything she can to make sure she has a close relationship with her grand-daughters, to give them something to remember her by.

The book has inspired the national Legacy Project. The project offers families free online activity kits, guides, tip sheets, resources, contests, workshops, and more to build and main-tain close bonds and celebrate the important legacies passed down from generation to generation (for more information, visit www.legacyproject.org or call 1-800-772-7765).

So, maybe you're wondering how to get started. Maybe you'd like to be closer to your grandchildren and adult children. Maybe you're new to grandparenting and uncertain about it or over-whelmed by it. Maybe you didn't have a loving grandparent role model yourself, or are unlike your "old style" grandparents and are wondering how to recreate the role to suit you. Whatever your situation, you can build a strong, loving grandparent connec-tion in your life. Poet William Stafford once said that the power of stories is that they are about "discovering what the world is trying to be." I want to help you discover the grandparent you can be. All you have to do to get started is follow five simple steps.

If you build it, they will come.

*"Grandparents can do more for us
than anyone else in the world;
they sprinkle stardust in our eyes."*

Alex Haley

Why Grandparents Are VIPs

NEVER DOUBT THAT YOU are a very important person – a VIP – in your grandchild's life. Anthropologist Margaret Mead once even stated that connections between the generations are "essential for the mental health and stability of a nation."

A couple of decades ago, grandparents had a more "hands-off" attitude. They didn't feel it was their place to be too involved with grandchildren. They didn't want to "meddle." Now we realize the value of the grandparent/grandchild relationship. In today's busy, two-career and single-parent families, an involved grandparent can go a long way to filling a void for children. In extreme situations, the courts have found it's often a grandparent who can reach a troubled teen when no one else can.

On a lighter note, a teacher friend of mine had her grade four students talk about their heroes one day in class. One girl said her grandmother was her hero. When the teacher asked why, the girl explained, "Because she's the only one in the whole world who can boss my parents around!" Grandparents can also be depended on to give kids the real scoop. One girl told me, "My grandma is the person who tells me things about my parents they would rather I didn't know."

I remember seeing a T-shirt available in both children's and adult sizes: "When the going gets tough, I go to Grandma's." Ask many adults – men and women – to recall a couple of fond memories from childhood, and most often one of the memories will involve a grandmother. It's a very important, special relationship for people, one that can give them strength and comfort far into adulthood. Said one woman in her forties, "Gram has always been a strong, stable force in my life. She's my compass. There's north, south, east, west, and Gram."

The special kind of love you get from a grandparent is a love you can't get anywhere else. A relationship with a grandparent is often freer and far less psychologically complex than with a parent. The grandparent/grandchild relationship is second in emotional importance only to the parent/child relationship. Just ask a child! One study of school-aged children found that if they were in charge of family vacations, their first choice would be to go to... grandma/grandpa's house – "because it's fun."

I've seen it in my workshops and in all the research: relationships between young and old, between grandparents and grandchildren, make us feel connected. They make us feel connected not only to each other, but to something bigger – to the flow of life, to the past and to the future. And this connection leads to very real, tangible benefits for grandchildren, grandparents, and parents.

Benefits to Grandchildren

The benefits to children of a close connection to their grandparents include:

- Children have a better sense of who they are and where they've come from.

- Children develop higher self-esteem, better emotional and social skills (including an ability to withstand peer pressure), and can even have better grades in school.

- Children feel special. They're "spoiled" a little. Believe it or not, research shows this is a good thing. Most grandparents don't have to play the role of provider or disciplinarian, like a parent does. Children know that being with their grandparents is special. They don't expect the rest of the world to treat them the way their grandparents do, so it's really not "spoiling." A grandparent's love is the unconditional stuff of fairy tales. One girl explained it this way: "Grandparents are great because they don't always tell you what you're doing wrong. They just like what you do, any way you do it."

- Grandparents can give children an undivided time and attention that tired, busy parents often can't. A six-year-old girl told me, "I love my grandma because she's always happy for me to show her things other people don't bother with." Another girl said, "Every time I go shopping with Mom she goes fast and says hurry up, hurry up. But when I visit with Grandma and go shopping, she always has plenty of time and lets me look at whatever I want to."

- Children have someone to talk with and confide in. While children want to be different from their parents, they often don't mind being like their grandparents. That gives grandparents a lot of power and ability to influence a troubled or confused child. One girl told me, "Granny fills the gap Mommy and Daddy leave out." A teenager told me that she can tell her grandmother things she would never, ever tell her mother. "My grandmother understands me," she said.

- Through sharing in a grandparent's interests, skills, and hobbies, children are introduced to new activities and ideas. Grandparents can be very patient, effective teachers. Knowledge, skills, and attitudes children pick up from grandparents tend to stick with them through life more than those picked up from other sources.

- Children learn firsthand about older people and aren't as susceptible to stereotypes. In one study, 62% of the children said they learned about older people from their grandparents. The grandparent/ grandchild relationship is a great place to start building positive attitudes toward aging and older people. There was a boy whose attitude about his grandmother was right on: "My Grandma may look old on the outside, but she's just like me on the inside." Another study showed that gang kids who have a close relationship with a grandparent are less likely to victimize an elderly person. They have more respect for older people.

Benefits to Grandparents

The benefits to grandparents of a close connection to their grandchildren include:

- Grandparents say they feel a "joyful freedom" in their new role. There's a saying that a mother truly becomes a grandmother the day she stops noticing all the terrible things her children do because she's so enchanted with all the wonderful things her grandchildren do. As a grandparent, you get all the benefits and joys of parenthood without any of the drawbacks.

- Many people see grandparenthood as a "second chance." Maybe you weren't able to spend as much time with your own children as you would have liked, or made some mistakes you've now learned from. Grandchildren are a fresh start.

- Active grandparents live longer, healthier lives, with less memory loss and illness. Recent brain research indicates that as we get older, enriched and fulfilling environments may result in less neuron loss and the growth of new synapses. One 68-year-old grandmother said, "The mess, the noise, the clutter. It's wonderful to be grandparents! We don't have time to be old, or complain, or be sick."

- Active, involved grandparents consistently report less depression and higher degrees of life satisfaction and happiness.

- Our society doesn't tend to value older people. Getting old is considered "bad" (though hopefully that's starting to change). In each other, grandparents and grandchildren find validation and respect. Also keep in mind that while adults may enjoy talking about "modern" grandmothers, children's perceptions haven't changed much from the time we were kids. Whether grandma has gray hair or blonde hair, whether or not grandma works outside the home, grandma is special because she's grandma. Talk about unconditional love!

- Grandparents and grandchildren fulfill the role of student and teacher for each other, and it's not always the older person who does the teaching. Children like to feel needed, and they can teach their grandparents lots of things – like how to find some pretty cool stuff on the internet! Grandchildren also help you see the world anew again, through a child's eyes.

- Grandparents have an opportunity to leave a powerful legacy, to make a difference, to send a

message into the future through their grandchildren. The relationship can fulfill our need for
immortality.

Benefits to Parents

The benefits to parents when the "grand generation" is a part
of their lives and their children's lives are also clear.

Today's parents are often stressed out. An involved, caring
grandparent can give them someone to talk with – someone
who's "been there" but now, with the benefit of hindsight, can
help put issues into perspective. It's comforting for parents to
know that there are other adults who love their children. There is
also the tangible support of physical and financial help when it's
needed.

Many people say their relationship with their parents
improves when children enter the picture. For example, an overly
strict parent suddenly becomes a "softie" as a grandparent. Adult
children see their parents in a new light, and this can help heal
relationships.

Bottom line: most parents WANT grandparents to be involved
– not in a judgmental, meddling way, but in a loving, supportive
way.

An Important Note about Divorce

When people divorce, they need to recognize how important it is for their children to maintain close ties with grandparents. Grandparents can be a critical source of stability in a time of turmoil. They can spend time with children who are feeling confused and hurt; they can answer questions in a nonjudgmental way; they can provide reassurance (many young children feel a divorce is their fault).

During a divorce, it may be hard for parents because a grandparent is tied to your ex-spouse. But, for the good of your children, you have to separate your feelings about the grandparent from your feelings about your ex-spouse. And grandparents, if you want to maintain your role, you have to be careful not to take sides.

This is one of the most challenging, difficult situations parents and grandparents can face. But, it's also the kind of character-building situation that if handled well, will prevent you from having regrets later.

A Note about Stepgrandparents

In today's changing families, stepgrandparents often wonder whether they have a role in children's lives. The answer is a qualified "yes." You have to consider the age of the children, any existing relationships with other grandparents, and your relationship with the parent/stepparent.

You will need patience to build a relationship with stepgrandchildren, and you will need to show love and support in a noncompetitive way. Seek *friendship* first, and take it from there. Children will always respond to an adult who takes an interest in them and gives them time and genuine attention. Don't underestimate your role in making a positive difference in a child's life.

A Note about Volunteer Grandparents

Many children don't have biological grandparents in their lives. There are more and more intergenerational programs springing up across the country that pair these children with older people ("surrogate" grandparents) in the community.

If you don't have grandchildren, this is a great opportunity to make a connection with the young. If you have grandchildren who live far away, consider also being a volunteer grandparent to a local child. You can keep in touch with your own grandchildren's interests, vocabulary, and development by simply being around children their age.

Virtually all of the benefits for children and grandparents discussed above apply in volunteer grandparent relationships. As I spoke to one girl about her volunteer grandmother, she said,

"She's my real grandmother because she cares about me. Spending time with her is one of my favorite things to do." Now there's a description of a VIP if I ever heard one!

*"Uncles, and aunts, and cousins, are all
very well, and fathers and mothers
are not to be despised; but a
grandmother is worth them all."*

Fanny Fern, *Folly As It Flies* (1868)

The 5 Steps to Building the Grandma (and Grandpa) Connection

THERE ARE FIVE SIMPLE STEPS to building the grandparent connection:

1. Feel It
2. Think About It
3. Plan It
4. Make Time For It
5. Enjoy It!

An Important Note for Grandfathers: Why do I focus on the "grandma connection?" Despite all the changes in society, women still tend to be the kinkeepers in families. They often take the lead in establishing close bonds with grandchildren. But, I don't want grandfathers to feel left out! There are many caring grandfathers, and all the information that follows will work for you too. Grandfathers can – and should – be actively involved with their grandchildren.

1. Feel It

"I'm a flower, poa, a flower
opening and reaching for the sun.
You are the sun, grandma,
you are the sun in my life."

Kitty Tsui
"Poa Poa Is Living Breathing Light"

There are quite a few grandparenting books out there. They're filled with lists and labels, tips and tricks, dos and don'ts. Often, they aren't the best place to start. They're too much about what's in your head and not enough about what's in your heart.

The grandparent connection has to start with your heart: how do you FEEL about being a grandparent? You need to feel how important the grandparent/grandchild relationship is, and explore the powerful emotions around it, before you can do anything else.

Start with Story

Stories are a powerful way to get to your head through your heart. I begin my Grandma Connection Workshops by reading my 32-page, illustrated storybook *Something to Remember Me By* out loud.

The book was inspired by my grandmother. My grandmother ("Baba," as I called her in Ukrainian) had a little ritual of giving me a small keepsake every once in a while and saying, "here's something to remember me by" – which is where the book's title comes from.

Something to Remember Me By is a story for both adults and children about love and legacies across generations. It tells the tale of the special relationship between a grandmother and granddaughter over the years. The story begins with the happy times and "big, warm smiles and warm, snuggly hugs" they share. They do simple things together like bake cookies, read stories, play games, do errands, and cuddle in front of the television. Many visits end as the grandmother gives her little granddaughter a small keepsake as "something to remember me by" – a wooden doll, an old coin, a fancy pen you use with special ink. As the years pass, the grandmother grows older. It's the grown granddaughter who then gives back to her grandmother. In the end, it's clear that young and old have something very special to give each other, and the most important gift we can all give is our love.

You can read *Something to Remember Me By* on your own, and share and discuss it with your adult child or your grandchild. It's a short book, but an emotionally powerful one. From the story's text to the richly-detailed watercolor artwork, it gets straight to the heart of the grandma connection. It helps you understand how the relationship develops, how important it is to a child, and how meaningful it can be to an adult. As the emotions well up, you can see yourself in the story. In my workshops, I can actually see the moment that people GET it! You have to feel it to live it, and a story has tremendous power to help you feel it.

As you read articles and other stories about grandparents (see the Great Books & Resources section), monitor how you're feeling. Be honest. Exploring all your feelings now gives you a strong foundation for building a close, honest relationship with your grandchildren. Some general questions to ponder:

- What do you think you "should" be feeling about grandparenthood? Why? One of the big myths about grandparenting is that it comes naturally. It comes no more naturally than being a parent. It's something that evolves and that you grow into. Don't feel badly if you don't have it "all figured out" right from the start. No one does!

- Are you excited about being a grandmother? Why or why not?

- How do you feel about your "baby" having a baby?

- Imagine holding your newborn grandchild. How do you feel?

- What are your worries about being a grandmother?

- How do you feel about getting "old"? Grandparenthood is one of those life transitions that cause us to pause and take stock of where we're at. It's natural to feel some sadness. A part of your life is over. But a new part is also beginning. Accepting your mixed feelings in a nonjudgmental way gives them less power to get in the way of your relationship with your grandchildren. It allows you to give your love freely. This is also an opportunity to make sure that you'll have few regrets at the end of your life. What do you still want to do in your life?

- Do you feel being a grandmother is important? Why or why not? Are you willing to make it a priority in your life?

- How would you like your grandchildren to feel about you? To create the illustrations for *Something to Remember Me By*, we had to search for a woman to be a model for the grandmother character in the story. We finally narrowed it down to a handful of finalists and showed photographs of the women to groups of children. The children didn't care about the women's weight, hair color, wrinkles, or any of the other things that we feel make us look "old." The "grandmother" they chose was the one they most wanted to give a hug! That's what the grandma connection is all about.

The 5 Life Lessons of Grandparenthood section can help you explore these questions further.

Write a Letter

Another good way to explore your feelings is to write a "love letter" to your grandmother (even though she may be long gone) about what you got – or didn't get – from the relationship. If you didn't have a grandmother, write to an imaginary one (perhaps a character you've seen in a movie or on television, or someone you've read about).

In your letter, you want to cover it all, the positive and the negative. Be persistent. You may think you have nothing to say about some of the suggested questions below, but after some thought, you may find that all kinds of memories and feelings well up.

Come to understand your grandmother, or your idea of a grandmother. In turn, you come to better understand yourself.

Here are some questions you can cover in your letter:

- What kind of clothes did your grandmother wear?

- What were her hands like? Her face? Her eyes? Her body? How did she smell? How did she talk?

- What did you call her? What did she call you?

- How did your grandmother care for her house (inside and outside)? What do you remember about her cooking? How did this relate to her values or upbringing?

- What part of her house was your favorite?

- How often did you see her? What kinds of things did you do with her?

- Do you remember anything funny that happened?

- Did she ever scold you? How? What happened?

- Was there ever a time your grandmother frightened or embarrassed you? Why do you think she did it (did she have a good intention)? What did you learn from it?

- What did she feel strongly about? Did she have moral, political, or spiritual views that influenced you?

- What significant life events happened to her?

- What kind of advice did she give you? How did she word it?

- Did your grandmother have any illnesses? How did she deal with them?

- How did other members of your family view your grandmother? Can you remember a specific incident that demonstrates her role or place in the family? How did people outside the family view her?

- In what ways are you like your grandmother? How are you different?

- Do you still think about your grandmother? When? What is your single most vivid memory?

- Did your grandmother give you any keepsakes or special photos? What's the story behind them? Why are they important to you?

- How did your grandmother die? Were you there? What did it mean to you? How would you have liked it to be different?

- Is there something you never said to your grandmother that you would like to?

- If you could wish for anything, what would you wish for your grandmother? For you? For your children and grandchildren?

2. *Think About It*

> *"What families have in common
> the world around is that they are the
> place where people learn who they are
> and how to be that way."*
>
> Jean Illsley Clarke, *Self-Esteem*

The grandmother role model many immediately seem to think of is Barbara Bush. "Modern" grandmas that also come up are Florence Henderson, Priscilla Presley, and Goldie Hawn. For grandfathers, Bill Cosby's name often pops up. Other famous grandpas include Mick Jagger, Pierce Brosnan, and Billy Crystal.

What kind of grandparent do you want to be? Don't feel boxed in by the stereotypes. You don't necessarily have to cook or knit to be a grandmother. Give some thought to what's right for you.

Create Your Own Role

You can be any kind of grandparent you want to be. There are no rules. Your role can range from Cookie-baking Grandma to Rollerblading Nan. It's the love and time you put into the relationship that counts. Exactly HOW you do it is up to you.

Here are some questions to consider:

- What meaning does grandparenthood have for you? How do you think your role in your grandchild's life is important?

- What would you like to be called – grandma, gran, gram, grammy, nana, nan, nanny, abuela, baba, bubbe, mimi, omi, nonno? The list is limited only by your heritage and imagination. Keep in mind that while you might have negative (i.e. "old") connotations with a name like "grandma," children won't carry the same associations with the name. They'll love you for you!

- What are your interests, talents, skills, hobbies? How do you plan to share them with your grandchild? It's interesting to note that some studies show certain genetic traits may actually skip a generation. For example, your daughter may not be artistic, but you and your grandchild may share a talent for art.

- How much time do you plan to spend with your grandchildren? Are you willing to juggle your schedule to make them a priority?

- What are your resources? What do you want to contribute financially, physically, and otherwise to your grandchild's upbringing?

- How much help do you want to offer parents? How do you feel about babysitting?

- What are your values? What family traditions are important to you?

- What aspects of your heritage do you want to pass on to your grandchild? Note that if your adult child has married someone of a different race, faith, or culture, you must start by facing any of your own feelings and prejudices about the differences. Then discuss the issue with your adult child. Sharing your racial, religious, and cultural identity with your grandchild, while at the same time showing tolerance and acceptance of differences, helps your grandchild grow into a better person. It also prepares them to be a part of an increasingly smaller world.

- What else do you want to pass down to your grandchildren?

- How do you want to contribute to your grandchild's development? For example, in addition to giving gifts that are purely for enjoyment, you may also want to make it a priority to give educational books, games, and computer software that will expand your grandchild's horizons.

- How do you want your grandchildren to remember you? As fun and silly? As full of life? As a good listener? As showing interest and concern? As giving them a sense of their roots? As providing love and security? Think about the memories you want them to carry forward into their adult lives, to their children and grandchildren.

As you think about your role as a grandparent, keep one fundamental principle in mind: you are NOT your grandchild's parent. You are not in charge. That role belongs to your adult children, and you must respect that – and them. Now that your adult children are parents themselves, your relationship with them will change. Ideally, it becomes more "adult/adult" – although you are still their parents, and there will inevitably be times when they will need your (nonjudgmental) love and support. And you are, of course, still a VIP in your grandchild's life!

After pondering all these issues, you might want to summarize your thoughts by writing a concise grandparenting mission statement for yourself.

Do Some Research

When most people do something important in their lives, like become parents or buy a house, they usually do a little research.

Grandparenting is no different. There are some great grandparenting books and resources listed at the back of this book that will help you be the best grandparent you can be. They cover topics ranging from brushing up on current childrearing practices (you can also look at recent parenting books) to childproofing your home to dealing with various legal issues.

As part of your research, find grandparent role models you like. Look in books, in advertisements, to television and movies. Look at your friends and acquaintances. It's easier to start with a role model and adapt it as you go along.

Talk to Your Adult Children

Once you've had a chance to think about your role and do some research, it's also important to talk with your adult children about the kind of grandparent you would like to be.

Share your hopes and fears, and talk about expectations – yours and theirs. Be empathetic and respectful of their views. By talking about your role before a grandchild is born, you pave the way for a smoother relationship over the long term. Everyone starts on the same page. Parents are the gatekeepers to grandchildren; if you have a good relationship with them, chances are much better that you'll have a good relationship with your grandchildren.

A conversation with your adult children also gives them reassurance. They're trying to find their way in the new, often overwhelming role of parents. Both you and they will make mistakes along the way. You will probably "push each other's buttons" at times. Mistakes are fine; they are part of living and learning. But, you are older and, hopefully, wiser. You can provide a leadership role in many ways. Make sure that small mistakes don't become bigger than they need to be or adversely affect your relationship with your children and grandchildren. Above all, what you want to emphasize – to yourself and them – is that you're all on the same side. You want to build a strong, loving, supportive, happy family.

3. Plan It

> *"In the years since I began following the ways of*
> *my grandmothers I have come to value the teachings,*
> *stories, and daily examples of living which they*
> *shared with me. I pity the younger girls of the future*
> *who will miss out on meeting some of these fine women."*
>
> Beverly Hungry Wolf, *The Ways of My Grandmothers*

How are you going to build a close, loving, lifelong relationship with your grandchildren?

Nothing in this hectic world happens without a plan, and relationships are no different. Relationships today are complicated by busy schedules, divorce, and families spread across the country. You have to make sure the grandparent connection happens.

Two Keys for a Connection

When you're planning the kinds of things you're going to do to establish and maintain a loving relationship with your grandchildren, keep two key factors in mind. Research shows that a real bond develops when there is:

1) **Regular contact** – you need to have frequent, consistent contact with your grandchildren. If

you're nearby, that means seeing them at least every week or so. If you live far away, that means seeing them as often as possible, and having weekly contact by phone, mail, and e-mail. Grandchildren need to feel that you're accessible and that they can count on you when they need you.

2) **Emotional attachment** – you and your grandchildren need to feel close to each other. That means you have to get to know your grandchildren as people – their personality, their likes and dislikes, their interests, etc. And grandchildren need to get to know you as a person. You have to be more than cardboard cutouts to each other. It's important here to stress that you need to start as soon as your grandchild is born (some grandparents are even in the delivery room, but this is a very individual choice). Close bonds are best established when children are young.

Planning a close, loving relationship with your grandchildren also involves their parents. **Parents have a critical role to play in building the connection between grandparents and grandchildren.** Children need to feel that their relationship with their grandparents is directly supported and encouraged by their parents. Parents need to make it easy for grandparents to have regular contact with their grandchildren. Bottom line: all three generations have a responsibility in building family bonds.

Putting All the Pieces Together

Exactly what shape your plan takes depends on the kind of grandparent you've decided you want to be (in step 2). There are as many different plans and strategies as there are grandparents.

You'll find lots of ideas to get you started in the Tons of Terrific Tips section of this book. For example, if you're a long-distance grandparent, you can talk with parents to arrange a mutually convenient time for a regular phone date with your grandchildren. If you live close to your grandchildren, perhaps part of your plan will be to make every Thursday night your night to take them to a local pizza place.

Being a long-distance grandparent involves a bit more planning and creativity than if you live near your grandchildren. But, in either case, you have to have a conscious plan to be a part of your grandchildren's lives. I know one set of grandparents who live in the same small city as their grandchildren, but haven't made the time to see them for two years. Remember: whether you live nearby or not, the rewards of being more than a "birthday gift" grandma are significant to both you and your grandchildren.

Your plan will evolve as you get to feel more comfortable in your role, as you get to know your grandchildren, and as they grow older. It can combine the best of old, treasured family traditions with the "newest, coolest" things that "modern" grandparents and grandchildren do together. Keep in mind that you should be realistic in your expectations, and flexible in your plan. One of the biggest traps you can fall into is, "This wasn't the way it was supposed to be." It will be what it will be. Your goal is to adapt your plan in a positive way that continues to build a loving connection with your grandchildren.

4. Make Time For It

> *"What you're going to hear from people is,*
> *'We don't have the time.' But if you don't have the*
> *time for one night or at least one hour during the week*
> *where everybody can come together as a family,*
> *then the family is not the priority."*
>
> Oprah Winfrey

Time is the most limited resource in today's world – and the one your grandchildren need most. It can be hard for grandparents who have busy schedules and may still be working. But putting time into your relationship with your grandchildren is the difference that makes the difference. Children carry the legacy not only of what you give them, but also the void that's left by what you don't.

It's the Simple Stuff

When I'm feeling down, it's my grandmother's memory that gives me strength. One of my favorite memories of my grandmother is a little tradition we had on my birthday. Every birthday, she would get up very early and be the first to phone me and sing "Happy Birthday." She'd be so pleased that she beat everyone else to it! To this day, in my mind, I can still hear her singing "Happy Birthday." It's the little things you remember, the time someone took to make you feel special.

The more complicated the world gets, the more the little things, the simple things matter. In *Something to Remember Me By*, the grandmother and granddaughter play games and read stories together, spend time in the kitchen, do errands, and cuddle in front of the television. Anyone can do these things, but the problem is that most people don't take the time. Many grandparents think they have to do big, fancy things with their grandchildren. But it's the simple things that make memories, and build the connection.

I remember a workshop I did with a mixed group of grandparents and grandchildren. A young boy was there with his grandmother. His grandfather had died recently. I asked the boy what his best memory was of his grandfather. He said, "the chocolate bar." His grandmother looked puzzled. She didn't have a clue what the boy was talking about. As it turned out, the boy's best memory was a chocolate bar he, his grandpa, and his grandma had shared sitting on the edge of a water fountain in a shopping mall. Such a small thing. The grandmother had forgotten all about it. When I asked the boy why this was his best memory, he replied simply, "Because it makes me happy."

Children need you. They need your love, your attention, and your time. They need the big, warm smiles and the warm, snuggly hugs. The seemingly small moments of today will be the memories of tomorrow. And even the simple rituals you establish, like my grandmother's birthday telephone call or waving "good-bye" from the same window after a visit, add to a special connection that will transcend time.

Set Your Priorities

You are of a certain generation. You probably have many roles and identities in your life. You've finished raising your children. You've worked hard. You have your own personal interests, goals, and values. And now you have to make time for the next generation.

Some people can hardly wait to be grandparents. Others are more hesitant. When you finally become a grandparent, it's often not something you have much control over. You don't make the decision. Grandchildren arrive when they arrive! What you do have control over is how you choose to make them a part of your life.

Grandparenthood is an opportunity to reassess your life. Are your grandchildren one of your priorities? Take an interest in the next generation by getting involved with them. Focus on the present and build toward the future. Put time into creating good experiences and memories, for your grandchildren and by extension your adult children. This can be a time to mend broken relationships and strengthen existing ones. Be a model for the possibilities of life. This is one of your big chances to make a big impact on the future.

5. Enjoy It!

> *"Life is no brief candle to me. It is a sort of splendid*
> *torch which I've got hold of for the moment,*
> *and I want to make it burn as brightly as possible*
> *before handing it on to future generations."*
>
> George Bernard Shaw

We give new mothers baby showers, so why not do something for new grandmothers? Grandparenthood is a major life transition, and if you don't do something to mark it, it tends to be devalued. Rites of passage give meaning and purpose to life transitions. Your transition into grandparenthood deserves some sort of recognition.

Grandma Needs to Party!

We end my Grandma Connection Workshops with a big party. Grandmothers get VIP buttons and a specially signed keepsake edition of *Something to Remember Me By* to share with their grandchildren.

I think grandma showers are a great idea. Friends can gather together to celebrate the arrival of a new grandchild. Family parties that include and celebrate the grandparents are also a nice way to mark this life transition.

If you aren't the party type, then come up with your own way of celebrating grandparenthood. Do something that has meaning for you. You can have a picnic with your spouse to share your feelings and memories. You can write a letter or poem to your new grandchild and save it to pass along to them when they're older. You can plant a tree. You can even pamper yourself with a day at the spa! Whatever you do, you need to do something that says, "I'm a grandmother, and it's GREAT!"

Celebrate the Process

Being a grandparent brings many moments of tremendous joy. But, like anything important in life, it also brings moments of frustration and worry. Starting a journal about your experiences and feelings is a wonderful way to grow as a grandparent, and a nice keepsake to pass along to your children and grandchildren. It is both a form of reflection and celebration.

Speaking of celebration, why not celebrate Grandparents Day? It falls on the first Sunday in September after Labor Day. In 1978, President Jimmy Carter first proclaimed this day of celebration for grandparents. Although it hasn't caught on with florists and card companies (which really isn't what holidays are supposed to be about anyway), that's no reason that you and your family can't take time to mark the occasion.

Finally, don't forget to be silly. When we're children, we're silly and joyful and playful much of the time. As we grow up and try to make our way in a complex world, we have to act like "adults." Parenthood is largely a serious responsibility – although parents are allowed brief moments of indulgence when you can relive childhood joys, like "helping" your children play with that train set you always wanted! As a grandparent, you're now at a place in your life where you've established yourself psychologically and can afford to be silly for much of the time. Be spontaneous, inventive, and imaginative with your grandchildren. Make faces and big messes, get down on your hands and knees, and laugh until it hurts. Be joyful! Not only will you and your grandchildren have a great time together, but it will help keep you young – guaranteed.

*"Grandparents need grandchildren to
keep the changing world alive for them.
And grandchildren need grandparents to
help them know who they are and give them
a sense of human experience in a world they
cannot know. Here is a model for mutual
learning across generations."*

Margaret Mead

Tons of Terrific Tips for Grandparents Near and Far

MAYBE IT'S BEEN AWHILE since you've been around young children. Maybe being a grandparent is brand new to you and you need all the insights you can get. Maybe you're facing some frustrations and just need some new ideas. Whatever your situation, here are some tips, for grandparents near and far, that you can use as guidelines, reminders, and inspiration for building a loving, lasting connection with your grandchildren.

The pages that follow contain terrific tips for everything from visiting and playing with your grandchildren, to sharing life stories, to giving gifts and keepsakes. For even more ideas, tips, and free activity kits, as well as contests and other resources for grandparents, parents, and children, check out the award-winning national Legacy Project. Visit www.legacyproject.org or call 1-800-772-7765.

Tips for Visits

Visits are an ideal way to maintain the regular contact that's so important to building a close bond between grandparents and grandchildren. During visits, make sure you have as much one-on-one, "alone" time (i.e. without parents) with each of your grandchildren as possible. This can even be something as simple as, if the whole family goes for a walk together, walking a few steps ahead with your grandchild as the parents stroll behind.

Babysitting

This is a big issue for parents and grandparents. The bottom line: babysitting is NOT an obligation of grandparenthood. It is okay to say "no." You may have limitations of time, energy, and physical ability. Your adult children should respect these limits.

That being said, family is about helping each other. If you can babysit, it's a chance to get to know your grandchildren and help your adult children at the same time. Parents face so many stresses. Think back to when you were a parent. Wouldn't you have appreciated a helping hand? Offering to help out by babysitting provides both physical and emotional support.

Babysitting is one of those topics you should discuss with parents when you're going through step 2 (thinking about your role). By talking about it and setting expectations up front, you'll have a smoother relationship over the long term. Some factors to think about when you're setting babysitting expectations:

- How much babysitting do you feel is reasonable?

- What days of the week are best for you? Are you willing to babysit overnight? Evenings? Afternoons only? Are you willing to help out in a pinch and be called at the last minute?

- What are your personal preferences? For example, you might prefer to babysit when your grand-children are awake so that you can spend quality time with them. You can't get to know your grandchildren if they're sleeping!

- If you're babysitting regularly while parents are working, do you wish to be paid? If you don't want money, is there some other way you would like to be compensated?

- Would you prefer to go to your children's house – which is already stocked with childcare equipment and toys – or are you willing to equip your own house?

- What information do you need from the parents
  (e.g. food preferences/allergies, emergency phone
  numbers for doctors, etc.)?

Regular Dates

Grandchildren need frequent, consistent contact with you
(see step 3). If you live nearby, try to set at least one regular date a
week with your grandchildren – perhaps a play date with younger
ones, and a pizza date with older ones. For long-distance grandparents, talk with parents about a good day and time for a regular
weekly phone date with your grandchildren. Telephone "visiting"
(see Tips for Talking), in addition to regular letters and e-mail, is
almost as good as the real thing.

Individual Outings

It's important to spend time with each grandchild one-on-one,
away from siblings and parents. A simple walk to the neighbor-
hood playground is a good start. Then try a day trip to the museum, zoo, or amusement park. If you work outside the home, you
might take your grandchild to work with you for a day (many
businesses have "bring your child to work" days). Perhaps it can
be your responsibility to take your grandchild to a regular sport-
ing activity they're involved in. You could also arrange for music

or sports lessons for your grandchild (of their choosing of course!) and take them to those.

Special Days

Try to be with your grandchildren on special days, like their birthday or a recital. The fact that you make the effort to be there counts as much as being there.

When you visit with grandchildren, why not make some days a special "holiday" just for the two of you? Invent an event – red and blue day (you both wear only red and blue clothing); lemonade day (make and sell lemonade to neighbors); Lego day (spend the day making a Lego city); bubble day (experiment with bubbles of all kinds); pillow fight day (come armed and ready for a specified hour of fun).

Setting Ground Rules

If you live near your adult children and grandchildren, talk about the rules for visits. Will you have a key to each other's homes? Do you feel comfortable just dropping in on each other, or do you expect a phone call beforehand? Your adult children may not want you to drop in at mealtime or bedtime, and you may not want your grandchildren over when you've planned a quiet evening.

Be respectful of rules your adult children set for their children. For example, many parents want to limit their children's intake of sugar, salt, and fatty foods. Remember: you are not your grandchild's parent!

When grandchildren are visiting you in your home, it's okay to set house rules. You can even involve older grandchildren in developing and writing out the rules so that they'll take more ownership of them. Some examples of rules: take off your shoes before walking on the carpet; eating in the family room is okay, but no eating in the living room; no red, purple, or orange drinks in the house (which can stain badly); no hitting, pinching, or kicking; if you want something, begin with "please"; etc.

Since you're a grandparent (and grandparenting is supposed to be fun!), why not have some fun rules in addition to the serious ones? See if your grandchildren can remember to always hop three times before they enter the kitchen, open all doors with their left hand only, say the entire alphabet before they sit anywhere in the house (chair or floor), or do seven jumping jacks each time the phone rings.

Extended Visits

Particularly for grandparents who live thousands of miles away from grandchildren, longer visits may be the only way you get to see each other. But, you don't want a visit to be too long; it puts a lot of strain on regular routines and schedules (whether you're visiting them or vice versa).

To start, three days (a long weekend) is a good amount of time for a visit. This leaves everyone wanting more! You can then evaluate how feasible a longer visit is – one week, two weeks, or more – depending on the people and temperaments involved, guest accommodations available, schedules, etc.

A tip for bargain hunters: many airlines offer special last-minute, internet-only fares to selected destinations at discounts of as much as 75%. You have to be flexible though (and do warn your adult children that you're coming!).

Visits in Their Home

When you're visiting your adult children's home, especially if it's an extended visit, remember: it's not your house and you are not in charge. Respect their space, their way of doing things, their schedule. Other tips:

- It's a good idea to let your adult children know up front about any special needs you have, like dietary restrictions or physical limitations.

- Don't expect grandchildren to spend every minute

with you. Even young children are often involved in
many activities and have a regular schedule. Try not
to feel hurt. If you don't push or make grandchildren and their parents feel guilty, they will *want*
to spend time with you.

- It's nice to give parents a break and offer to babysit
  for at least a couple of hours at some point in the
  visit (this also gives you "alone" time with your
  grandchildren).

- If you want to help with cooking or cleaning, make
  the offer and let your adult children take the lead in
  telling you what to do, how to do it, and when to
  do it.

- Leave something behind so that good memories of
  your visit will linger – a clever note hidden some-
  where in the house, or even a batch of homemade
  soup in the freezer.

Visits in Your Home

I was about eight years old and fascinated by lipstick. During a
visit to one of my grandmothers, I made a very large (but very
artistic!) lipstick smear on the carpet by her bed. Even though I
got in serious trouble from my parents, the very next week I went

to my other grandmother's house and did exactly the same thing! My grandmother's almost saintly response? "Children will be children." That was one of the things I loved about her – she rarely yelled at me.

The *idea* of grandchildren can often be less messy than the reality. But that's also half the fun! Particularly if you're planning to have your grandchildren over for an extended visit, here are some key tips to help things run smoothly:

- Be realistic in your expectations. Children sometimes get sick; children don't sit through dinner; your house will be a mess; you will be tired.

- It's okay to set house rules (see Setting Ground Rules above).

- Childproof your home. Get down on all fours to look at the safety of your home from a child's perspective. Major safety concerns: keep the floor, tabletops, and counters clear of all breakables or potentially dangerous items including knick-knacks, books, wastebaskets, and small appliances; make sure there are no small objects lying around that a child can swallow and choke on (e.g. pens, coins, buttons, paper clips, etc.); put away plastics such as dry cleaning or trash bags; put plastic safety covers over unused electrical outlets; get rid of dangling electrical cords; secure drapery and blind pulls out of reach; put all poisonous materials out of reach (including houseplants); make sure your hot water isn't hot enough to scald; put up folding gates to keep children away from stairs and out of "off limits" areas; put safety latches on cabinets in the kitchen, bathroom, and workshop; secure any loose rugs; block or lock windows so that children can't open them and fall out; keep the toilet seat and lid down and install a toilet seat latch; put corner guards on sharp edges like coffee tables or fireplaces; have basic first-aid items handy (you can buy prepared kits that store neatly).

- Don't have plans to do other things during a visit. This is your time with your grandchildren. Put all your energy, time, and attention into it.

- Preparation is important. Start by talking to parents and grandchildren in advance about what they'd like to do; don't assume you know.

- Be sensitive to trying to maintain your grandchildren's familiar routines (e.g. mealtimes, bedtime). This helps prevent them from becoming overstimulated or overtired.

- Plan a couple of big, fun things to do.

- Involve your grandchildren in your life and in the things you like to do, whether it's decoupage, gardening, horseback riding, woodworking, or computers. You can even become the grandparent that "specializes" in a certain activity (e.g. one grandmother might focus on sharing her love of sewing, while the other might focus on sharing her love of music). This way your grandchildren get to know you, and you can introduce them to new experiences which may turn into shared interests.

- Have toys, art materials, videos, storybooks, etc. handy for when you need to distract your grand-children or fill some time.

- Make sure your grandchildren have a chance for some physical activity each day (ideally, outdoors) to burn off energy.

- Don't overschedule. It's also important just to "hang out" together. For example, grandparents are living time machines. Children love "old stuff," and they will often enjoy just looking through a drawer at old, interesting, or unusual things. Explore your attic, basement, or closets together.

- If having more than one grandchild visit at a time is too much for you, plan individual visits. This can become an exciting, anticipated event for everyone. For example, one grandmother who has five grandchildren (living in different parts of the country) set the expectation that each grandchild, when they reach the age of eight, gets to come and spend a special week visiting with her all by themselves.

- Believe it or not, you'll probably miss your grandchildren when they leave. Give yourself time to rest, but also make sure you have something planned – like an outing with your friends – to help you get over the "grandchild blues."

Vacations

Perhaps you'd like to take your grandchild on a vacation – just the two of you! For a young child, staying at a motel with a swimming pool for the weekend can be a great adventure. With children eight and up, going camping or on a boat cruise will make lots of memories. There are even special camps and vacation packages for grandparents and grandchildren. By taking a vacation together, you get to spend time with your grandchild and get the added advantage of seeing the world through a child's eyes.

Get Support from Your Friends

To make visits or vacations easier, you can involve your friends and their grandchildren. Make it a group affair. For example, if your grandchildren are visiting for an extended period and you're feeling tired or overwhelmed, plan one day with other grandparents and grandchildren. This gives you a break and some support. If you introduce your grandchildren to your friends and their grandchildren, this also includes them in your social circle and helps build a stronger connection.

Tips for The Kitchen

Everyone loves the first watercolor illustration in *Something to Remember Me By*. It's a big, sunny, bright, warm kitchen in which you see the grandmother and her granddaughter. People say it looks "exactly" like their grandmother's kitchen!

Research shows it's not the living room or dining room that's the best place to make a cozy connection with your grandchildren. It's the kitchen. Both adults and children tend to be most relaxed and receptive in the kitchen. We smell and taste in the kitchen; we talk about and learn things in the kitchen.

Many grandmother memories have to do with food. People remember a special dish their grandmother made, or the great food she cooked on special occasions. Some memories involve grandparents letting you have foods your parents wouldn't. One man told me about Sunday dinners at his grandmother's house. She wasn't a great cook, but she always made him his favorite dish – mashed potatoes with canned spaghetti on top! He said his mother thought it was disgusting. But his grandmother said that if that's what he wanted, that's what he'd get.

A Special Place

To make your grandchild feel at home in your kitchen, consider some personal touches:

- A place mat just for them – perhaps with their name on it.

- A cup with your grandchild's name or photo on it.

- Nonbreakable, child-size cutlery and plates.

- A special seat at the table reserved for your grandchild when they visit.

- A drawer full of paper, crayons, and small toys that they can use and keep things in.

- A cupboard that your grandchild is allowed to go into all by themselves to get snacks.

- And don't forget to proudly display any photographs or artwork from your grandchild on your refrigerator or bulletin board.

Treats

Part of the fun of being a grandparent is being able to indulge your grandchildren in treats of candy and "junk" food. But many parents today want to limit their children's intake of sugar, salt, and fatty foods. Respect their wishes, but also try to negotiate a reasonable plan with parents for occasional treats. If you can't come to a compromise, be creative with nutritious treats, like juice popsicles or baked apples.

Making Food Together

When you and your grandchild cook together, your grandchild gets your undivided attention, you help teach them an important skill, you help build their self-esteem ("I can cook too!"), and you both enjoy the benefit of something edible at the end. Some ideas:

- Baking cookies is an all-time favorite. Kids love the dough, it's easy, and it's tasty. If you're not a baker, then use a mix or the premade, frozen dough. It's the time you spend together that counts.

- If you want a change from cookies (perhaps a "healthier" alternative), try making pretzels. Soften 1 package of yeast in 1½ cups of lukewarm water. Add ¾ teaspoon salt and 1½ teaspoons sugar. Mix in 4 cups of flour, and knead the mixture into a soft, smooth dough. Cut the dough into small pieces. Your grandchild can then roll and mold the pretzel dough into alphabet letters (spelling their name), animal outlines, building outlines, sculptures, or wild designs. In another bowl, beat an egg; then brush onto the pretzel shapes. If you use salt, sprinkle a dash of salt (preferably course grain) onto each pretzel. Bake the pretzels at 425 degrees for about 15 minutes, or until golden brown. Once the pretzels have cooled, then it's time for the taste test!

- Encourage your grandchild to help you make meals. A young grandchild can peel the banana for a fruit salad. An older grandchild can help with slicing, dicing, shredding, or mashing the potatoes. Give them a sense of involvement in what you're preparing by asking for their opinion with questions like, "Do you think this might need a bit more lemon juice?"

- Children enjoy stuffing almost anything, whether it's cheese into celery, or pureed vegetables into a baked potato skin.

- Your grandchild will get a lot of enjoyment and pride out of taking the lead in making you both a "whole meal." Start with something simple like a peanut butter and jam sandwich. Sandwiches are easy to make as well as an opportunity to be creative.

- If you're a long-distance grandparent, write down simple recipes and send them to older grand-children. With some help from parents, they can follow the recipe and report back to you.

Other Kitchen Fun

Kitchens aren't just for eating. Here are some non-food ideas:

- Kitchens are a treasure trove of containers of various sizes to sort and compare, pots to bang with a wooden spoon, plastic containers to fill with beans, a dustpan and brush to learn to sweep, and so on. While making it clear to your grandchildren that some cupboards are out-of-bounds, you might consider keeping a special cupboard of kitchen items just for play.

- There are plenty of musical opportunities in the kitchen. For example, take two paper or styrofoam cups and fill one of the cups a quarter to half full with uncooked rice. Place the empty cup on top of the full one so that the rims align. Tape them together securely. Now you and your grandchild have a great maraca!

- You and your grandchild can use food items to

make things. String pasta on a piece of yarn or string to make bracelets, necklaces, and headbands. You can even dye the pasta with food coloring before assembling. Have a variety of pasta on hand – tubes, stars, pinwheels, etc. You can also make great pasta collages, or macaroni greeting cards (macaroni glued on heavy paper or cardboard to spell words or make pictures).

Family Meals

A shared, sit-down meal provides a sense of belonging. It's a chance to bring all three generations in your family closer.

In today's busy world, time is one of the greatest gifts you can give. Preparing a home-cooked meal goes a long way to winning your grandchild's heart and your adult child's undying appreciation. If you don't have the time or energy to make a meal from scratch, buy everyone's preprepared favorites, heat them up, set a nice table, and enjoy!

Tips for Playing

Children will often wander about asking, "Will you play with me?" When an adult actually says yes, it's like winning the lottery! When you play with your grandchildren, you show them that what's important to them is important to you.

Play is serious business to children. From the time they're born, children have a universal need to play. It's how they learn and grow. Playing with your grandchildren is not only fun, it gives you a glimpse into their world. It's a key way for you to learn about them. You gain insights into their unique personality and temperament, find out about their likes and dislikes, and come to understand how to respond to their phase of development. Playing is also a precious opportunity to relive your own sensory experiences, and explore the world as if for the first time.

The Basics

Give your grandchild your complete attention when you're playing with them, and keep these tips in mind:

- Respect children's play. Let your grandchild take the lead in what they want to play with you. Give them your undivided attention and, at the same time, observe them. When they're "into it," never interrupt the flow without a good reason.

- Be wary of safety considerations, particularly when children start to get overexcited.

- Have a special drawer or box in your house filled with age-appropriate books, games, toys, and puzzles. Stock up on crayons and paper, coloring books, connect-the-dots books, stickers, and even junk mail, catalogs and magazines that children can cut up. Grandchildren love knowing you have special things just for them, and look forward to playing with these things when they visit you.

- For babies and young children, play consists of tickling games, peek-a-boo and patty-cake, reflections in the mirror, copying each other's facial expressions, blowing bubbles, stacking blocks, exploring shapes, and playing with a ball. Games are simple, like ones that involve taking turns, "Now me... now you."

- As children grow older, they're interested in things like board games, puzzles, puppets, magic tricks, and sophisticated building sets. You can make a theater together from a large box and put on a play or a magic show. You can create a Lego city in your living room. All kinds of craft activities are also popular with children.

- Make-believe is great play. Children love a small little world of their own – a playhouse, a tent, a tree house, chairs with a sheet thrown over them. Build cardboard houses together from boxes. Make crowns from thin cardboard, decorate them with paint and sparkles, and play "King (or Queen) of the Castle."

- Have a dress-up box of items you can both try on. It can include old clothes, tablecloths, strips of fabric, artificial flowers, large feathers, hats, shawls, scarves, neckties, shoes, purses, and costume jewelry.

Bath Play

Bath time is extra special, particularly for babies and younger children. Don't rush it. Let children splash and explore with water toys. Washing should be secondary to playing! A safety reminder: NEVER leave a child unattended in a bath, even for a moment.

One idea for long-distance grandparents is to send a special rubber ducky or other bath toy that your grandchildren can play with each day so that you can "be with them" at bath time. Parents can refer to it as "grandma's ducky" to help build the connection.

Music

Children love music and singing. You can sing children's songs with your grandchildren and have CDs around the house to play when they visit. You can also introduce them to some of your favorite songs. How about "Rock Around the Clock" for some dancing in the kitchen, or Louis Armstrong's "What a Wonderful World" before bed? Older children will be fascinated by your "old-time" record collection and player (for playing with only when grandparents are supervising, of course!).

Making Things Together

Grandparents teaching grandchildren to make things is a great cooperative activity. It can extend over several visits and become a project, like building a birdhouse, learning to sew, or knitting a scarf.

Arts and crafts activities are always winners. Try things like painting, making clay figures, or creating collages by cutting fabric pieces or magazine pictures and pasting them on paper.

Whatever you're making, always collect everything you need ahead of time so your grandchild isn't frustrated waiting. They just want to get into it! Go through an activity step-by-step, at the child's pace. If it's a messy activity and the weather is warm, consider doing it outside to make cleanup easier.

Science Fun

When I run mixed workshops with grandparents and grandchildren, I've found science activities to be a great way to bridge the generation gap. You're never too young or too old to explore the wonders of the world around you.

I've written a book titled *Science Is...: A Source Book of Fascinating Facts, Projects and Activities*. It's huge – filled with over 450 activities, projects, games, puzzles, and stories. You don't need any background in science, and you can use readily-available, inexpensive materials. Most of the time you'll be having so much fun that you won't believe you're doing "science." Learn how to make gigantic bubbles or a mini volcano; put on a play that shows what happens to a hamburger when you swallow it; go stargazing; do a bee dance. The book also has lots of fascinating facts your grandchildren will love – did you know that a cockroach can live for nine days without its head?

Secret Signals

Create your own playful "secret" signals, for grandparents and grandchildren only. How about a secret handshake when you see each other? For example, you could do a double shake (standard handshake done twice, quickly); triple snap (snap fingers three times); high five (hand and palm up, clap together); double cross (shake opposite hands at the same time).

Tips for Photographs

The cover of *Something to Remember Me By* is an illustration of a pile of photographs (grandmother and granddaughter playfully rubbing noses, grandmother holding her newborn granddaughter, grandmother and granddaughter sharing a secret, and so on). A special photograph even plays a pivotal role later in the story.

Photographs carry a lot of emotion and meaning for adults, and even young children respond to photographs. Starting at about two, children will show a spontaneous interest in photos you have framed or sitting around the house. And their interest doesn't wane; they're as happy to look at photos for the seventh time as they were for the first time.

Photos (and Videos) of You

Lots of photographs of you should be around grandchildren in their home, particularly if you're a long-distance grandparent.

Keep a steady stream coming of recent photos of you doing whatever you do as a part of your life. You can also regularly send videos of yourself. The key to sending a video is to keep it brief (children have short attention spans) and entertaining (talk to your grandchild as if they're with you in person, and don't be afraid to be goofy).

Other tips for photos of you:

- Make up a large (at least 8×10), close-up photo-graph of yourself. Put it in a nice frame that can be placed on a table or hung in your young grand-child's room. Parents have a role to play here in pointing out the photo and telling a child who it is. Even pre-vocal children will begin to recognize your face and name. Parents can even make you a part of the bedtime ritual, by walking over to the photo to say "good night to grandma."

- A related note: babies have a very good sense of smell. When you send a photo, send along a sachet with your favorite perfume or hand cream. Your young grandchild will come to recognize your smell.

- Have your photo put on a nonbreakable cup or bowl. If your face is at the bottom of a bowl, your grandkids can eat their food to "uncover" grandma.

- If you're travelling, make an extra set of photos so that your older grandchildren can share in your adventures. You can even paste the photos on a large sheet of paper with captions about your trip.

- If you're the "stay at home" type, take photos (or have someone take them) of you during a typical day. "A Day in the Life of Grandma" can then be made into an album – and become a keepsake.

Photos (and Videos) of Them

Particularly if you live far away, encourage parents to regularly send you LOTS of photos of your grandchildren. Drop subtle hints by sending film, or a disposable camera. You want to watch your grandchildren grow up.

Part of being a grandparent is showering your grandchildren with attention. Taking photos or video of them is not only something you can use to "brag" with to your friends, but also makes your grandchildren feel important and special. They become the "star." Some tips and ideas:

- Have an "aim and shoot" camera ready at all times to capture spontaneous moments.

- Make a double set of prints for your grandchildren and their parents.

- Have a special grandchild bulletin board with photos of them as well as their artwork, newspaper clippings about their achievements, etc.

- Years ago, making silhouettes was very popular. You can take this special "photo" of your grandchild. It's an activity you can do together, a way to make them feel special, and it can become a keepsake. Have your grandchild sit sideways in front of a blank wall with a large sheet of white paper taped to it. Make the room dark and use a bright light or flashlight to cast a shadow of their profile onto the wall. Using a pencil, trace around the shadow to draw the profile on the paper. Then, put the white sheet of paper with the profile on top of a sheet of black construction paper. Cut along the profile, through both sheets of paper. The black silhouette looks great pasted onto white paper and framed.

Photocopy Old Photos

Every so often, photocopy a few old family photographs and give or mail them to your grandchildren. Focus on "people" pictures rather than "place" pictures – photos of you in your youth, your children when they were young, relatives, etc. Write a brief caption underneath each photo explaining who's in it, when it was taken, and what's going on. This gives your grandchildren a sense of their family history.

Photo Parties

Here are three kinds of photo "parties" you can have:

- When you're visiting with your grandchildren, going

through old photo albums is always fun. You can have regular photo parties in which you look at old photos and then take some new photos immediately afterward (perhaps even recreating poses). Looking at photos is a great communication activity: "I remember when this was taken..." It's not fancy or high tech, but it works. Children will often want to look at the same photos again and again. But, be sensitive to the limited attention spans of younger children, and allow grandchildren to take the lead in asking questions about what interests them.

- You and your grandchildren can have another kind of regular party in which you make something with photos (or photocopies of photos). For example, you can help your grandchild make a collage of photos of things the two of you have done together.

- Have a family photo party. Children, parents, and grandparents can each choose their favorite family photos. Everyone can work together to lay them out in a scrapbook and decorate themed pages. It's a great way to organize those photo packets we all have scattered around the house, recall family memories, and create a treasured keepsake.

Tips for Writing

Phone calls, videotape, audiotape, and e-mail are effective for building the grandparent connection. Computers, in particular, offer you instantaneous communication on a daily basis. You can e-mail a joke a day and other messages, or even play games together online.

But nothing beats writing something down on paper. Writing a letter, for example, is not only a form of communication, but it becomes a permanent record for the future. Letters can also be read and reread.

You can start writing to grandchildren around age two, when most begin to use language. Writing is a good way to build a close connection, and you also serve as a model to help your grandchildren develop this critical communication skill.

Postcards

Children LOVE to get mail! It makes them feel important and gives them something to look forward to. So use the mail connection with grandchildren near and far.

Postcards are an easy, fun way to get into a pattern of writing that doesn't take a lot of your time. Get a big pile of bright postcards with interesting pictures (you can collect postcards in card shops, specialty shops, gift shops at museums, and during your travels). Then, mail a postcard a week (even to grandchildren who live nearby) with a short note about the picture, something you've done over that week, or something you're thinking about the grandchild. For example, "Dear Lindsay, I thought you might like this picture of an owl. Owls are awake during the night and sleep during the day. I saw an owl when we were hiking last week. Look at the big, yellow eyes the owl has! Can you open your eyes as wide as the owl's? Lots of love, Grandma."

Write Letters

Occasional letters are fun for grandchildren who live nearby (remember, children love mail!), and regular letters are a key way to build a connection over long distances. Here are some tips to get you started:

- Write letters about what's going on in your life: something that happened in your house, at work, on your street, while you were shopping, during an exercise class; something that happened with a pet or other animal; things you've done with your grandchild; experiences from your childhood or your children's youth; anticipation of happy events.

- Make letters an appropriate length for the age of

your grandchild, and be conscious of using words they'll understand. For very young children, focus on one main thought and include pictures (hand-drawn or clipped from magazines).

- When you write a letter, don't: push for skills beyond a child's capabilities ("Kathy can say the whole alphabet, can you?"); exert subtle pressure ("I would really like you to come to my house for Christmas"); invoke guilt or have a disciplinary tone ("I don't like it when you do that"); or divide a child's loyalties ("Do you love me more than your other grandmother?"). You can acknowledge sad events ("I'm sorry to hear that your dog died"), but don't dwell on tragedy.

- Be creative with letters. Include simple, hand-drawn pictures, or cartoons you've clipped out of the newspaper. You could create a cartoon character and have an ongoing comic strip for your grand-children.

- Poems and word games are always an interesting addition. For example, make up a poem or a list of special attributes with each of the letters in your grandchild's name.

- There are greeting cards on the market (or you can

make your own using heavy paper) that have a front panel with a line-drawing picture children can color. You can write a brief note inside the card, and ask your grandchild to color the picture and return the card to you.

- To make letters even more fun, cut them into pieces (not too small!) that your grandchild can put back together like a puzzle. Some specialty stores sell blank puzzles that you can write on, break into pieces, and mail.

- To encourage your grandchildren to reciprocate, ask directly that they answer your letters. Ask some specific questions to get them thinking. Younger children can draw pictures; older ones can write about what they're up to.

- Make a photocopy of your letters. It's likely that your grandchildren won't hold on to them (they're not at the sentimental stage yet). When they get older, a scrapbook full of your letters becomes a treasured keepsake.

- Do something special with your letters to make them immediately recognizable as "something from grandma." For example, you can consistently use a red envelope.

Help Grandchildren Write Letters

One way to increase the likelihood that your grandchildren will write to you is to teach them the skill of letter writing by helping them write letters to other people. You can help them enter contests, write to famous people (e.g. stars, politicians), or write to people they've gotten to know through you (like the grandchildren of your friends).

Write Stories

Try your hand at writing stories especially for and about your grandchildren. Make them the "star." Some ideas:

- Use your grandchild's name often, and include the names of friends, pets, and other family members.

- You can write a "Once upon a time..." imaginative story, or a story based on an event that actually happened. Children love stories about their own achievements and familiar situations, objects, people, and pets.

- Include descriptions of what's happening, as well as the feelings of the characters.

- Keep the language simple, and don't put too many sentences on one page.

- Be as creative as you want to be, drawing your own pictures, clipping pictures out of a magazine, or using photographs.

- You can put your story into book form, using different sizes, shapes, and colors – a long, thin book; a round book; a big, yellow banana book; a red apple book with a little stem.

Family Newsletter

Become the editor of your own family newsletter. It's a great way to build a connection between all generations. Everyone in the family keeps up-to-date on the family news, and everyone gets the news at the same time. You don't have to feel pressured to follow a regular schedule; get out an issue as often as you can. Make it a simple, cut-and-paste affair, or you can get fancy on a computer. Some ideas for content:

- Share happy events in your life, your adult children's, and your grandchildren's.

- Use headlines that proudly proclaim your grand-children's achievements: Ben hits home run! Sarah loses first tooth!

- Cover the results of whatever your grandchildren

are up to – from the latest "toilet paper tube" bowling tournament to a Scrabble contest.

- Encourage grandchildren to write stories or draw pictures. Older grandchildren can write articles, perhaps surveying family members for their opinions about "hot" issues (like family meals, toys, recycling projects, etc.) or interviewing parents and grandparents to collect family stories.

- You can have an "I remember when..." column in which you share reminiscences.

- You can have an advice column – "Ask Grandma."

- You can include contests, jokes, and a "quote of the month."

- Also include tidbits about family history or important dates in the family (e.g. September 20 is Janice's 4th birthday; June 25 would have been your great-grandparent's wedding anniversary).

- As editor, try to be fair and diplomatic; give everyone the same amount of space.

When a newsletter issue is complete, make one master copy and photocopy additional copies (be sure to put a copy away for posterity).

Journals

Starting a personal journal is a good keepsake for both your children and grandchildren. It becomes a permanent record. Children and grandchildren can read it when they're ready and interested. Some things you can include:

- Experiences from your present life, including times shared with your grandchildren that you want them to think about and remember.

- Memories from the past, including experiences from your childhood and young adulthood. Describe how your experiences are similar to and/or different from your grandchildren's.

- Anticipation and then review of happy events (like an extended visit with your grandchildren).

- Stories about your children's youth, and about your parents and grandparents. These help your grandchildren understand their roots, and teaches them about the value of life experiences.

- Hopes for the future – for your children, grandchildren, and great-grandchildren.

Make sure you write not only about events themselves, but about your feelings. Write simply and clearly. Try not to take a moralistic tone, and don't "write down" to your grandchildren. You can do drafts before you put the final entry, in its final form, into the "good" book.

Another journal idea is to have an annual travelling family journal – "A Year in the Life of Our Family." Grandparents, parents, and children each do a section in a shared journal and send it back and forth through the mail. It's like you're writing a book together. Each household has the journal for perhaps a month. People write about what they're thinking and doing. You can include drawings, stories about events and activities, notes about ideas or thoughts. People can comment on previous entries. All generations participate, and it's like a "snapshot" of your family at a moment in time. The collection of annual journals will become a very important family keepsake.

Tips for Listening

Should a grandparent "just" listen? Shouldn't you dash in, take charge of the problem and, with your years of wisdom and experience, fix it? Well, not exactly.

As the old saying goes, you have two ears and only one mouth so that you can listen more than you talk. More than anything else in the world, all human beings – adults and children – want someone to listen to them. It is a fundamental need. People don't want or need your advice (unless they specifically ask for it and are ready to hear it). They want and need to talk about their problems. They need psychological air. They need to feel respected and understood. That's the way we get perspective on our problems.

Learning how to be a really good listener is THE most important thing you can do as a grandparent. It is the most precious gift you can give your grandchildren and your adult children. When you listen and give someone your understanding and support, you help them and you help your relationship.

Children are strongly influenced by what happens to them in their first five years. By age five, their listening patterns are established. If they are to feel respected, and to learn to listen and respect listening, they must be introduced to it in their family.

Engaging in good listening not only helps you build a close connection with your grandchildren, but it models effective listening skills and helps your grandchildren develop this essential communication skill.

Effective Listening

It takes empathy, skill, and self-control to listen well. As a grandparent, you are older and, hopefully, wiser. Listening well is your chance to demonstrate your wisdom.

To listen with genuine interest is truly emotionally supportive, even when you have nothing else to give. Here are some general reminders that are useful for listening to your grandchildren and your adult children:

- Don't just focus on skills. Both adults and children will pick up on it. Effective listening is based on how authentic you are. Do you REALLY care?

- Don't rush in with advice, comments, or solutions – even if they seem obvious.

- Don't criticize, moralize, or psychoanalyze.

- Don't interrupt or change the subject.

- Don't immediately start thinking about your response or rebuttal. If you're worried you're going to forget a key point, jot it down quickly on a piece of paper for later (but don't interrupt the flow of the conversation).

- Keep an open mind.

- Focus your full attention on what's being said. Ignore any distractions around you.

- Look behind the words, emotions, personality, or other distractions for the real meaning of what the person is saying. Don't let emotion-laden words throw you. Focus your attention on the central ideas and feelings.

- Look at what's being said nonverbally (e.g. facial expressions, eye contact, tone of voice, hand gestures, position of arms, etc.). Does the nonverbal contradict or support the verbal?

- Show you're listening through brief verbal expressions (e.g. "hmm" or "uh-huh" or "I see" or "right") and nonverbal acknowledgements (e.g. nodding your head, opening your eyes slightly, making eye contact, reaching out with your hand).

- Start by just being a sounding board. Open the door with phrases like "Do you want to tell me about it?" or "I'd like to hear what you're thinking."

Let the other person "get it all off their chest," and bounce ideas and feelings off you. Then start to...

- Reflect back what you're hearing to make people feel heard and understood: "Are you saying that...?" or "So you feel like...?"

- Ask questions to clarify for understanding, but don't interrogate. Ask simple questions like "What happened?" and "How did you feel?" and "What are you going to do?" and "Is there anything else you might do?" and "Is there anything I can do?"

- Be sure to avoid stock phrases that discount a person's perspective and feelings: "It's not that bad" or "You'll feel better tomorrow" or "Don't be so upset" or "You shouldn't feel that way."

- Above all, accept your adult children and grand-children for who they are.

Know When NOT to Listen

When emotions are high – yours or theirs – listening may not happen despite your best intentions. You can take a break and come back to the discussion at another time. Or, you can say that you want to listen, but that you're feeling very emotional at the moment. For example, "I have to admit that as much as I want to listen to what you have to say, I'm feeling a little defensive right now." A "headline" phrase might also help you to feel more in control and ready to listen: "I'm surprised and hurt to hear you say that. I don't know if I can agree with you, but tell me more about how you see it."

Listening to Your Grandchildren

Childrearing practices come and go, but common sense is always in style. Listening to your grandchildren is just a common sense way to learn about and understand them. Some special tips for listening to your grandchildren:

- Let your grandchildren have their say in their own words and at their own pace. Be patient.

- Don't make light of a problem or their feelings.

- Don't fall into the trap of telling them how you dealt with similar problems when you were their age. There will be other times for your personal stories from the past. This is the time to be in the present by focussing completely on your grandchild's thoughts and feelings.

- Never be critical of their parents, and don't try to "fix" the problem (it may not even be within your role as a grandparent, especially if it involves a conflict between a child and their parents – don't get caught in the middle!).

- Once your grandchild has had their say, put your emphasis on expressing your understanding and empathy for what they've said and how they're feeling. Some positive messages you may want to communicate both verbally and nonverbally: I like you just the way you are; I like spending time with you; I'm interested in what you're doing, thinking, and feeling; I won't judge or criticize you; I'm proud of you; you can count on me.

- Often when children talk, they want you to respond to the feeling rather than the content of what they're saying. For example, your little grand-daughter may ask, "Will there be big kids at the party?" You would be responding to the content by saying, "No, all the kids at the party will be about your age." It's better to respond to the feeling behind the content by asking, "Are you nervous about the party?"

Grandchild Confidences

To build a relationship based on honesty and trust, you should honor your grandchildren's confidences. You need to earn their respect.

If your grandchild has shared something with you that you're not sure they want you to talk about, check with them first. Even if you think it's just something "cute" or inconsequential, they may not see it the same way. By checking with them, you make them feel respected and allow them to make the choice. In the long run, they're more likely to come back to you with the big things.

If your grandchild has told you something that is potentially harmful or dangerous, you can try to find a way to alert the parents without breaking the confidence. Or, you can express your concerns to your grandchild and encourage them to go to the parents (you might even offer to be there for support).

Listening to Your Adult Children

The physical and emotional pressures on new parents are tremendous. There will be times when they feel completely overwhelmed and exhausted. As you're showering all your love and attention on your grandchildren, don't forget that their parents may be able to use a little too. This doesn't mean taking over or

giving advice; it means listening and being there in a loving way.
Some special tips for listening to your adult children:

- Ask your children what they need and what they
  want you to do; don't assume you know. Useful
  questions include: Is there any way I could help
  with that? What would you like me to do more of?
  What would you like me to do less of? Is there
  anything I've done that you would prefer I don't do
  again? Is there anything I don't do that you'd
  appreciate me doing? Is there anything you'd like
  me to do in a different way?

- Don't argue or protest about the answers or
  responses you get; go away and think about them
  honestly. They can give you a fresh perspective on
  your role in the family, and help you improve a
  relationship that's stuck or in a rut.

- Be sensitive to the situation. For example, a new
  mother just home from the hospital may not
  appreciate you coming over and monopolizing the
  baby. What she might appreciate is some help with
  the cooking, cleaning, and laundry (ask first, of
  course).

- In an emotional situation, such as an exhausted
  parent balancing the needs of two young children,

let listening be your lead into practical action. Start by listening to and acknowledging the feelings of frustration and exhaustion. Then move gently into suggesting some ways you can help, options from which the parent can choose: taking the baby (or the baby's sibling) for a few hours; paying for help with the house; doing the laundry; filling the freezer with a few precooked meals. In this way, the parent feels understood and in control (they get to choose the most helpful option).

Forgiveness

During an evening of babysitting, one couple was so upset by their grandchild's "disrespectful" behavior that they didn't speak to the parents or see the grandchild again for a year. No one wins in a situation like this. And without contact, you certainly lose any opportunity you might have had to positively influence your grandchildren.

Don't get stuck in your expectations – the way your relationship, your grandchildren, or your adult children "should" be. Grudges damage relationships and souls. Forgiveness is key in family relationships. No family is perfect. You can always find a reason to justify your anger. Find a bigger reason to let go of it. Forgiving (though not necessarily forgetting) is not a sign of weakness, but of strength.

Never think your grandchildren don't know what's going on. Even young children pick up on tension. You can work to diffuse tension by listening and understanding. If you've been hurt by something that your adult children or grandchildren have said or done, try to take another perspective on the situation. Learn to live with your adult children's choices (even if you disagree with them). Don't punish your grandchildren for their parents' actions. Accept them for who they are. Work for compromise. And don't worry what other people think.

You also need the courage to bring up difficult topics for constructive discussion. If you're upset by something and make the judgment that it's too big or important to let go, then initiate a conversation. If your children or grandchildren have been hurt or offended by something you've done, have the courage to say, "I'd like to understand why you're angry with me" and then *really listen* to the response.

The Tips for Talking that follow will help you deal with difficult, sensitive discussions.

Tips for Talking

Before you read Tips for Talking, read the Tips for Listening above. Listening is always the first, best step for building relationships and resolving conflicts.

Grandparenting involves negotiating some tricky territory. You may have different values and priorities, or a different parenting style, than the parents of your grandchildren. For example, one common area of disagreement is discipline. It can be difficult to be an involved grandparent, yet not one that "meddles." You want to be able to talk about important issues, and yet respect the fact that you are not your grandchildren's parent.

Curb Criticism

Your expectation from the start should be that your children will raise their children differently than you raised them. If you go in with this perspective, it makes things much easier for everyone. Respect for your adult children's way of doing things is important; it's often what's missing when a grandparent is overly critical. Some tips for curbing criticism:

- It's the little comments that accumulate into a big problem. Don't comment on everything your grandchild or adult child does that you disagree with. Don't constantly make "helpful suggestions." Let most of the little things go.

- There's a difference between expressing your feelings and criticizing. You're criticizing if you say, "I think my grandson should be in bed now. It's much too late for a child to be up!" You're expressing your feelings if you say, "I worry that he isn't going to get enough sleep. Will he be too tired tomorrow?" Keep in mind though that too much "expressing" turns into criticism no matter how you word it.

- Try to be open and nondefensive in your interactions.

- If you say something that your children or grandchildren interpret as criticism, be prepared to apologize: "I'm sorry I sounded critical. I didn't mean to."

- NEVER criticize your adult children in front of their children. This only makes them feel hurt and defensive, and undermines their authority. Find a private moment to discuss issues.

- Decide what the big, important issues are to you.

Think about them carefully before bringing them up. If you still feel you must bring up an issue, then have a specific, focussed discussion about it rather than making random comments.

Some Advice on Advice

As a grandparent, you're entitled to your opinion – but not to meddle or manipulate. Don't play games. There is a fine line between showing your interest, being involved, expressing your wishes and needs, and being just plain overbearing. You can suggest in a nonjudgmental, supportive way. But the final decision isn't yours; it's the parents'. Accept parents' decisions with a smile and with grace. Realize that everyone has their opinions and their own way of doing things, and there are bound to be things you'd do differently.

Your goal is to create an open, honest, supportive communication environment (see Tips for Listening). Both your adult children and grandchildren are then more likely to come to you seeking advice (and they may even follow it!).

Resolving Conflicts with Your Adult Children

There may be times when you feel you need to discuss something important, but difficult or sensitive, with your adult children about your grandchildren. This takes thought and courage.

Most people don't like conflict because it's uncomfortable. But conflict can also be an opportunity to get everyone's feelings and ideas out on the table, come up with better ways of doing things, and make family relationships stronger. There are no guarantees, but much of it depends on how you handle the conflict. You can take a leadership role in handling conflict effectively.

Much of the information that follows is based on the work of the Harvard Negotiation Project (see the Books & Resources for Grandparents section). They've been involved in studying and resolving the full spectrum of conflicts, from international political crises to interpersonal disputes. Here are some key tips:

- Never have an important discussion in the heat of emotion. Walk away and think about the issue first. If, after you think about it, you decide that the issue is too big or important to let go, then initiate a conversation.

- When you're talking about something difficult or sensitive, a relaxed atmosphere helps. Find a neutral, private time, when things are calm. Sometimes, it's easier to have a chat with your adult child over a cup of coffee, or when you're doing routine things like folding laundry.

- Recognize that every conversation has three parts:
  1) What happened, who did what when, etc.
  2) Spoken and unspoken feelings – yours, theirs, and anyone else's involved (at their core, most difficult situations don't just *involve* feelings, they're *about* feelings).
  3) Your own internal talk about what's going on, whether you're handling it right, what the situation means to you, etc. (your internal talk affects how you respond to others and the situation, and how open you are to coming up with solutions).

- Don't go into a discussion by blaming, accusing, denying, interrogating, moralizing, lecturing, threatening, or shaming.

- Do remember that there's only one person you have complete control over: you. Make sure you start from an honest place. Despite what we sometimes pretend, we go into many conversations trying to prove a point (or ourselves right), to give someone a piece of our mind, or to get them to do something we want. Instead...

- Go into the discussion with an open attitude, one based on truly seeking FIRST to listen and understand the other's perspective. Put yourself in their shoes. THEN talk about your point of view. If you give someone a chance to talk first, and they feel listened to, they are far more willing to listen to you.

- Separate the people from the problem. Be soft on the people, hard on the problem. Empathize with and respect your adult children, even while you disagree with them. Particularly in a family, the relationship is more important than the substance of the conflict.

- Focus on interests, not positions. Don't focus on each other's "bottom line." Instead, explore perspectives and needs. Don't stay stuck on the surface, but get to the core of the problem. Ask "why?" and "why not?"

- When it's your turn to talk, use description. Describe your purpose rather than state your case. Describe your feelings: "I'm anxious about bringing this up, but at the same time, it's important to me that we talk about it." Use a three-part message structure that 1) describes behavior (When you...); 2) moves into feeling (I feel...); and 3) ends with effects (because...). For example, "When you cut the conversation short, I feel hurt because I don't feel part of my grandchild's life." Also, acknowledge and take responsibility for your part: "There are several things I've done that have made this situation harder."

- Once everyone has aired their views and feelings, move into inventing options for mutual gain. Try to come up with a number of creative, cooperative solutions. Quantity and variety count here, not quality; you can make a final decision later.

- When you come to making a final decision, try to use objective criteria to evaluate the options you've brainstormed. Be open to reason, and to ways other people in similar situations might have resolved the problem. Find a point of agreement to build on, rather than focussing on points of disagreement. If you've decided on some of your preferences, don't present one option as "the truth." Try to put choices on the table: "I can do this or I can do that. It's up to you to tell me which you'd prefer." Share why you've chosen certain preferences. Leave room for change and for good feelings to emerge.

If, despite your best efforts, you can't seem to resolve a critical issue, consider involving a mediator – a mutual family friend or a family counsellor. Mediation and negotiation are much better than, for example, going to court in serious situations. A court ruling doesn't bring you love or respect. You can't mandate those. Most intergenerational conflicts can be resolved in other ways.

Resolving Conflicts With Grandchildren

Depending on their age, you may also be able to use some of the above ideas for dealing with serious conflicts with your older grandchildren (i.e. teenagers, young adults).

Many conflicts with younger grandchildren involve discipline. If parents would like you to use a certain method of discipline, like a time-out, follow their preferences. But, in general, discipline is not your job; it's the parents' job. For grandparents, scolding is out, artfulness is in. Sometimes, particularly with young grandchildren, distraction with a splash of humor moves things along. You can also offer a "choice" to resolve a struggle: "Do you want to wear white socks or blue socks?"

If you're resolving a conflict between your young grandchildren (perhaps they're visiting with you and a ruckus erupts over a toy), it's always handy to keep the old standby "paper, scissors, rock" in mind. It's a playful way to decide who gets to do what, who gets to go first, what happens next, etc. The whole game is based on three hand positions: hand open flat is paper; two fingers out is scissors; and hand in a fist is rock. Each position is superior to one of the others and inferior to the remaining one: paper always covers rock; rock always dulls scissors; and scissors always cut paper. Grandchildren all make a fist, pump their hands up and down twice, and on the third pump show one of the three hand positions. If two people have the same hand position, repeat. Conflict resolved!

Telephone Talk

Research shows that whether they live across the country or just a few blocks away, grandparents are usually the first people children regularly talk with on the telephone. Grandparents help their grandchildren learn telephone skills and etiquette. Regular telephone talk, particularly between visits, is also a great way to build a close connection with your grandchildren. Some tips:

- You can start calling and talking to grandchildren as young as six months. They can just listen to your voice (you can sing a song, for example, as a parent holds the phone to your grandchild's ear). Use your grandchild's name often. They will get used to your voice and start responding to it.

- For young children, ask specific, but open-ended questions (i.e. ones that require more than a one word answer) to keep the conversation going. For example: what did you have for breakfast? what did you like about it? what did you play today? what was your favorite part of the movie? why? You can also tell them a bit about your life, like what you ate for breakfast! However, spend most of the conversation focussing on your grandchild's life rather than yours.

- If you're a long-distance grandparent, talk with parents about a good day of the week and time for a regular phone date with your grandchildren. If it's scheduled at a convenient time, it becomes something that everyone looks forward to. You can use the date to talk about things, or even to read a story to your grandchild (you might both have a copy of the same book so that your grandchild can turn the pages and see the pictures).

- If you ever call at an inconvenient time, try not to take it personally. Be gracious and offer to call at a better time.

- End your conversations with a kiss and a big telephone hug!

A special telephone note to parents: program "Grandma" into one of your telephone's speed-dial buttons. Let young children push the button to learn how to make an instant connection to grandma. For older children, allow them some freedom (depending on the telephone charges involved) to call grandparents whenever they like. Not only does this make a grandparent's day, but it gives children a sense of their power to keep in touch with their grandparents.

Talking with Your Grandchildren about "Kidstuff"

If you haven't been around children for a few years, you may feel it's a bit of a challenge to get a conversation going, in person or over the phone.

One good strategy for talking with children is to start with some interesting information or a fact, and then ask a question that ties the information to your grandchild's life. For example:

- In the ballet *The Nutcracker*, the Nutcracker is a toy soldier who comes alive and takes Clara on a wonderful trip. In the story *Pinocchio*, toymaker Geppetto makes a wooden puppet that comes alive. If you could choose one of your toys to come alive for a day, which would you choose? What would you do together?

- A human being's nose is very sensitive and can smell up to 10,000 different odors. An ordinary ant has five noses, and each nose smells a different odor. What's your favorite smell? Where do you smell it? What does it make you think of?

- Birds sing songs to warn other birds that there's trouble (like a cat nearby!), or to attract other birds, or just because they're happy. What's your favorite song? Why do you like it? Where did you learn it? Can you sing it to me right now?

Most adults enjoy a juicy tidbit in conversation, and children are no different. Little things your grandchildren will be interested in and that you can sprinkle into conversations include: nicknames you or their parents had; your favorite childhood games or toys; special places you liked to play as a child; your favorite subjects in school and why; your best teacher and why; your favorite sports team or personality; one of the first ways you earned money; commercial jingles you remember/like; your favorite dinner or food as a child.

As your grandchildren get older, you can arrange to watch certain television shows at the same time, or go to the same movie within a certain time period. This gives you a common topic and keeps you in touch with their interests.

Tips for Stories

I've seen the power of stories in the workshops I run with grandparents, parents, and children. Stories get to our heads through our hearts. They capture our imagination. They reach all ages and bridge the generation gap – you can pretend, discover, quiver, and laugh together. And each generation gets something slightly different from a given story, so stories can spark meaningful intergenerational dialogue.

There are two key ways you can use stories to build a connection with your grandchildren: sharing stories in books; sharing your own life stories.

Family Book Club

Start your own family book club with your grandchildren. Books are a way to reach out. They are gifts of love.

Whether you live near or far, once a month you can give or mail your grandchild a new book. If you're a long-distance grandparent and can't cuddle up to read books together in person, make a phone date to talk about books. With younger children, you can read a story over the phone while they flip through the pictures.

You can also send an audiotape of yourself reading a book.

Don't worry if you're not a world-class reader. You'll get better with practice. Feel free to add dramatic flair and be a ham. With the audiotape, your grandchild gets to know your voice, and can listen again and again. This kind of tape also comes in handy for parents, who may have to commute long distances. They can play it in the car to entertain children, and be building family bonds at the same time.

Reading Stories

Read all kinds of stories with your grandchildren (you'll find some great suggestions in the Books to Share with Your Grandchildren section). Reading a story together is one of the easiest, most powerful ways to build a close relationship. It takes some pressure off you to be entertaining or to say the "right thing." It's foolproof, cozy, and a natural way to start conversations.

Many parents today don't have as much time as they'd like to read to their children. Grandparents can fill this void. You can play a vital role in your grandchild's education. Children who are read stories are better learners and have stronger communication skills (i.e. listening, talking, writing, reading). Research also shows that by having contact with children's stories, which are often full of wonder and imagination, older people retain a better, happier outlook on life.

Reading stories aloud together (even with older children) will also give your grandchildren "something to remember you by." There was a man – a big, burly fellow – who came to one of my readings. He told me he loved his family getting together over the holidays because his father would read everyone – adults and children – stories. The children loved listening to their grandfather, but the man also admitted *he* loved listening to the stories. He said he loved the sound of his father's voice. Everything else left his mind when his father was reading – except for the loving sound of his father's voice.

As part of my Grandma Connection Workshops, I use my illustrated storybook *Something to Remember Me By* as an example to teach grandparents how to read a story. Here are the key tips:

- **Make stories a big part of your grandchildren's life:** Surround them with books of all kinds. Take them on frequent trips to the library and the bookstore. Let your grandchildren choose their own books, but also encourage them to try books they might not normally choose. Start your own family book club (see above).

- **The right story for the right time:** The times for stories are when a child has been energetic and is ready for a quiet activity, or at bedtime. Simple, repetitive stories with reassuring themes are best for reading before bed. More active or thought-provoking stories are better for a reading session during the day. Whenever you read, eliminate all distractions (e.g. TV, radio, phone, etc.) and focus just on your grandchild.

- **Cuddle, cuddle, cuddle:** Children need physical contact, and cuddling close while reading is a way to initiate this contact in a natural way. Find a comfortable chair or couch to cuddle up on. Don't forget to give an extra squeeze during scary or tender parts of a story.

- **Encourage active participation:** For very young children, even getting them to help turn a book's pages gets them more involved in the story. If there is repetition in the story, say these phrases together. If the story is a favorite one, let children finish familiar sentences. Have children count all the times a particular word appears on a page (e.g. and, the). If your grandchild is old enough to read, take turns reading parts of the story.

- **Read a story twice at one sitting:** Read a book the first time for a general sense of the words and the story. Then read it again to identify themes, to make connections from one part of the story to another, and to look more closely at the cover and illustrations. This is particularly important with older grandchildren. For example, in terms of themes in *Something to Remember Me By*, it may become clear only in the second reading that there is a subtle shift in the grandmother/granddaughter relationship as the story progresses. In the beginning, the grandmother gives to her young granddaughter; toward the end, when the grandmother is much older, the grown grand-daughter gives back to her grandmother (which is the theme of the give-and-take across generations). In terms of the illustrations in *Something to Remember Me By*, the cover of the book is an illustration of a pile of photographs. That same pile of photographs appears hidden in miniature in an illustration at the end of the story. At the beginning of the story, the young granddaughter makes a crayon drawing of her grandmother cooking soup at the stove. Years later, that same crayon drawing appears in a box of the grandmother's keepsakes when she is moving from her home.

- **Make "The End" of the story your beginning:** A story can bring up new ideas or difficult topics. It can start conversations in a natural way (children will be more receptive than if you try to force a conversation at another time). It can also be a bridge to sharing your memories. For example, because *Something to Remember Me By* is a story about the keepsakes a grandmother gives her granddaughter, many people tie it to keepsakes in their own life. You can share a personal story, and bring it alive by showing the keepsake – your mother's earrings, your grandpa's watch, an old train ticket.

- **Use a story as a creative experience:** Encourage your grandchild to use their imagination to fill in or extend a story. This develops their storytelling skills. For example, in *Something to Remember Me By*, the grandmother gives her granddaughter eleven gifts: wooden doll; stuffed bear; flute; coin; figurine; pen; watch; picture frame; tablecloth; heart cushion; cedar chest. Your grandchild (with a little help from you) can make up stories about each of the gifts. Where did each gift come from? How and why did the grandmother give her grand-daughter each gift? For example, maybe the coin came from a faraway country, an exotic country in which the grandmother was originally born.

- **Extend stories into your relationship:** Take parts of a story and make them a part of your relationship with your grandchild. For example, if you've read a book with nature themes, immediately plan to go on a walk with your grandchild to look for the flowers or birds from the story. Many grandparents are inspired to start a keepsake tradition with their grandchildren after reading *Something to Remember Me By*.

Telling Your Own Stories

Telling stories from your life helps your grandchildren get to know you and their family history. It gives them a sense of who they are and where they've come from. If you don't feel your storytelling skills are what you'd like them to be, some books to help you develop them are suggested in the Books & Resources for Grandparents section.

When you're telling your life stories, you don't want to make them too formal or do it all in one sitting. Weave your stories into everyday activities. Make them informal and natural. Tell appropriate stories at appropriate times. For example, you might tell a six-year-old about your first bike, while a teenager will be more interested in your first love. Other tips for telling life stories, as well as stories from your imagination:

- Children are interested in stories about your childhood and youth, as well as stories about their parents.

- If you're telling a story that involves a relative the child doesn't know or is dead, try to make the person more real using old photographs or keepsakes.

- Children like to hear about mistakes or bad decisions you made. But don't end with "the moral." Kids will get it.

- Try to let your stories be prompted naturally from a conversation, your grandchild's interest in a photograph or other object, an experience your grandchild has had, a book you've read together, or by a special holiday or other occurrence.

- A 15-minute story is long enough for children under five; five- to eight-year-olds can concentrate for a half hour or so.

- When you tell a story, make sure your grandchild is sitting comfortably, and encourage their participation. For example, they can repeat key phrases in the story. Also encourage questions; let your grandchild's interest lead your storytelling.

- Practice telling stories. One good technique is to tell the story by viewing it as a movie in your head and describing what you see, filling in as many details as possible.

- You need a strong start to capture a child's attention and imagination. Follow Cecil B. De Mille's advice to prospective filmmakers: start with an earthquake and gradually build up to a climax.

- Introduce each character in your story individually and vividly.

- Build up suspense until you get to the climax, and then tie up loose ends.

- Put your whole body into telling a story. Use facial expressions, gestures, and pauses. Vary your voice tones from whispers to strong accents.

- You can also bring stories alive using old photographs, keepsakes, articles of clothing, etc.

You can make a permanent record of your life stories by writing them down in a special book or journal (see Tips for Writing).

Tips for Gifts

Grandparents giving gifts is part of the magic of the grandparent/grandchild connection. You don't have to give big or expensive gifts to build a close, long-term connection. Gifts just need to be thoughtful and given with love.

The most important cautions are not to overwhelm your grandchild with too many gifts, try to buy their affection, or go against their parents' wishes. Never buy a big gift or one that will require special care or arrangements (e.g. pet, trip) without first consulting parents.

Gifts can stimulate your grandchild's imagination, entertain, educate, or just offer pure delight. In general, there are two kinds of gifts: the formal gifts you give for birthdays and special holidays; and the "little things" you give that make a grandchild feel special.

Toys

Children today have so many toys, many of which quickly become discarded or broken. Try to focus on toys with lasting value, or things children can use to be creative (e.g. art supplies, building sets, board games, a microscope). The more flexible and unstructured the toy is, the more lasting it tends to be.

It's okay to indulge children once in a while with a big, extravagant gift or a "fad" gift that a child just "has to have." But, consult with parents beforehand to make sure they don't have any strong objections.

Try to break the toy stereotypes. Don't just give girls dolls and boys trucks. There's one woman I know whose parents, when she was little, would never buy her a train set – despite her requests for one, Christmas after Christmas. Finally, it was grandma who took her seriously and bought her the set. She is now 47 years old, and still has and cherishes that train set.

Creative Gift Ideas

This is your chance to play detective (and get to really know your grandchild). What are your grandchild's interests or blooming talents? You can give gifts that encourage and support these interests and talents – tickets to events/plays/concerts; lessons; musical instruments; sports equipment; a magazine subscription; posters or paintings; calendars; educational, entertaining videos; computer software.

Keep a look out for special things to buy your grandchildren that "big kids" need – like a radio, clock, camera, desk, or bookcase. Bags for carrying things to school, for sports, or for travel are also a good idea.

Finally, books are always in style (see Books to Share with Your Grandchildren).

A note of caution: it's best to stay away from clothing because children's sizes and tastes are so variable.

Collectibles

Help your grandchild start a collection and then add to it over time. It can be cards of some sort (baseball to dinosaur), rocks, stamps, coins, comic books, miniatures or figurines, etc. There are also a variety of stickers and sticker book sets on the market that you can use with younger children. For example, you can give your grandchild an animal sticker book and buy packets of animal stickers over time for them to stick in the right spot and learn about animals. Whatever the collection, it becomes a common interest you can share with your grandchild.

Playful Gifts

One woman told me that during her four years in college she most looked forward to letters from her grandmother, which always contained a little "surprise" – a stick of gum, a cartoon clipped from the newspaper, a funny sticker, a lucky coin. You can give or mail your grandchild a little something every once in a while as a surprise. It's not the gift itself that's important, but the connection it makes. It says, "I'm thinking about you."

Send something small and inexpensive, perhaps once a month. You can start when your grandchild is around three years old. Craft shops and "dollar" stores are great places for these kinds of little gifts. Be creative and imaginative. You might send a finger puppet, small stencil, funny socks, a balloon with a message on it ("blow up this balloon to read a surprise message from grandma"), a musical toothbrush, a pen in the shape of a snake (there are some wild things in dollar stores!). You could also send things your grandchild can experiment with, like a magnifying glass, magnet, or flower/vegetable seeds.

Sometimes it's a nice idea to enclose a note with playful gifts suggesting things your grandchild can do. For example: "Here's a magnifying glass that's especially for you! If you hold it up to your eye and look through it, it makes things look bigger. Take it around the house and look closely at the fabric on chairs, the carpet, a banana peel. What do you see? Look at your brother's nose. Does it look bigger? Let me know what else you see with your magnifying glass."

Soap-of-the-Month Club

Have you noticed all the different sizes, shapes, fragrances, and colors of soap on the market? Keep your eyes peeled for different soaps during your regular shopping and during trips, gather together a collection, and then send your grandchildren a new little soap each month. Everybody needs to wash, so soap is something your grandchildren can use – and have fun with. They'll think of you every time they take a bath! Some other soap ideas:

- Make your own soaps to send your grandchildren. Mix 2-4 cups of soap flakes with ½-1 cup of water. Whip with an electric mixer, adding flakes or water as needed to get a mixture that has the consistency of cookie dough. You can shape the mixture into anything you want, roll it out and cut it with cookie cutters, or mold it in candy molds. Let the soap dry on wax paper.

- Melt glycerin and pour it into ice cube trays sprayed lightly with cooking oil spray. For added fun, drop in a coin or other tiny treasure. Let harden. Your grandchildren will be able to see through the soap and wash until they get to the treasure!

- You can take a plain bar of store-bought soap and use a knife or toothpick to carve in shapes and drawings, or even your grandchild's name.

Handmade Gifts

Something handmade makes a special gift in the present and can become a treasured keepsake over the years. You might make your grandchild a quilt, a special blanket, a sweater or scarf, a fancy T-shirt, a stuffed doll or bear, or doll clothes.

If sewing, knitting, or needlework is something new to you, you might start with a kit from a needlework or craft shop.

If you don't have the time or skill to make your grandchildren the "traditional" things, try your hand at more playful handmade crafts. It's the thought and creativity you put into it that counts. For example, make a picture out of pennies stuck to a sheet of colored cardboard (you can even spell out your grandchild's name). Children can admire the picture for a while, and then put the coins in their piggy bank. Another idea is to make shapes and animals out of the fuzzy "wire twisties" available in craft stores. You might make a giraffe out of a yellow twistie, and send it to your grandchild with another yellow twistie to playfully "challenge" them to make the same animal.

Money

Money is always welcome, even in small amounts. You just don't want it to be the only gift you give, or use it as a way to "buy" your grandchildren. My grandmother would often let me have the change after I went to the store for her, or would give me a dollar when I helped her out with something. It didn't happen all the time, and I didn't perceive it as payment for services rendered. I just felt special when she would give me "a little something" that was all my own.

You can be creative with money. For example, you can make the penny pictures described above. A roll of quarters can even be magic. Another twist is to give a grandchild a sum of money with the proviso that they give it away to a charity of their choosing. This can spark some good conversations with older grandchildren, teaches them about helping others, and helps them think about what they value and why.

If you choose to, you can do something bigger and fancier over time, like buying savings bonds or stocks, or contributing to your grandchild's college education. Instead of waiting until you're gone, you might also consider making it known to older grandchildren that you have money available for big wishes or needs, such as helping to buy a car or getting special medical treatment.

A word of caution: if you give money to your grandchildren, or to your adult children for your grandchildren, be careful about putting restrictions on its use. If you can afford it, and it's coming from your heart, give it – with the assumption that it will be used wisely. To do otherwise is to put a strain on your relationship.

Time

Time is the greatest gift of all. Time coupons are a creative way for both you and your grandchild to anticipate a fun, shared experience. They also give your grandchild some power in "redeeming" the coupon. You might have coupons for baking cookies, reading a story, going shopping, or learning how to do woodworking.

Final Gifts

How are you going to divide up your money and possessions – jewelry, pictures, family heirlooms? Arranging your estate in advance gives you an opportunity to think about the needs of your grandchildren (and children) and your hopes for them.

The one word of caution here is that you should discuss your plans with your adult children and your grandchildren (if they're old enough). This is the best way to make your intentions clear and prevent hurt feelings.

A Note about "Thank You" Notes

Parents have an important role to play in encouraging bonds between their children and grandparents. One of the easiest ways to do this is to help children write a simple "thank you" note for a gift from a grandparent. So many grandparents I talk to say this is

THE biggest complaint they have – they never get a "thank you" note. They often don't even know if a grandchild has received a gift safely, let alone whether or not they like it. If grandparents don't get feedback, how can they know what to get grandchildren?

A "thank you" note doesn't have to be fancy or long. It can just acknowledge receipt of the gift; have a line describing what the grandchild likes about the gift, or what they're going to do with it; and then end with a "thank you" and "I love you."

"Thank you" notes teach children an important social skill, and make grandparents feel loved and appreciated. They get two-way communication going.

What can a grandparent do to encourage "thank you" notes? You can talk to your adult children about how important acknowledgement is to you. You can also talk to your grandchildren and use this as an opportunity to teach a social grace. Explain that you want to hear from them and find out what they liked or didn't like about a gift. Be persistent in your communication, without anger or criticism. As a hint or reminder, some grandparents enclose a "fill-in-the-blanks" card they write out for grandchildren to return to them. Another good idea is to set an example yourself – acknowledge and thank grandchildren for something they've sent or given you, or even a phone call.

Tips for Keepsakes

One man told the story of visits to his grandmother's house when he was little and the cut crystal handles she had on the French doors into her dining room. His grandmother would take the door handles off, hang them on a string, and put them in the window so that the sunlight would catch them and there would be a rainbow in the room. When his grandmother died, his aunt gave him the door handles as a keepsake. After that, as he lived in different apartments and town houses across the country, he put those handles on either his bedroom door or the front closet door. Today, he owns his own home and the handles are on a prominent door. Sometimes, he and his six-year-old daughter take the handles off "to make a rainbow in the room." And that's the philosophy he takes to life, a philosophy he got from his grandmother: he's teaching his daughter that you can always find a rainbow when you need one.

You know when you hear a favorite song on the radio and your mind goes right back to a special memory? Keepsakes have that same kind of power. Grandchildren like the hottest new stuff, but they also have a real need for a sense of family history and connection. In the short term, keepsakes create an immediate sense of connection. Over the years, they become a powerful symbol of that connection. Keepsakes evoke memories and feelings. They also make us feel part of something bigger. They are a critical part of a living family legacy. Older people have a need to give keepsakes as "something to remember me by," and grandchildren have just as much of a need to receive them.

Many of the items discussed in earlier sections – like using photos/videos, keeping a journal, writing letters and stories for your grandchildren, writing your life story, giving a handmade gift – can become keepsakes. There are also some special things you can do with an eye toward creating keepsakes.

Something to Remember You By

Something to Remember Me By was inspired by my grandmother. She had a habit of giving me a small keepsake every once in a while and saying, "here's something to remember me by." Some of the keepsakes were things she made or bought; others were her own possessions. I have to admit I didn't like all the keepsakes at the time she gave them to me. There was one terribly tacky, flowery, orange and red and brown and blue tablecloth that was one of her favorites. I hated it! Today I look at that same tablecloth with a mixture of amusement and fondness. That's part of the power of keepsakes.

Think about slowly giving away some of your special possessions to older grandchildren (and your adult children) – cup and saucer sets, salt and pepper shakers, figurines, fine linens, old jewelry, cuff links, watches. Even if they don't fully appreciate the keepsakes now, they will in the future.

I've also heard some wonderful stories about people who buy special keepsakes or choose special possessions, wrap them up with a personal note, and hide them away in a closet or attic. Their plan is that when they pass away, their children and grandchildren will sort through their possessions and they will each find a package with their name on it as a source of comfort and remembrance.

One woman in New York told me she had lost both her mother and grandmother in the holocaust. She wanted to give her 14-year-old granddaughter a copy of *Something to Remember Me By* with some old photos and her grandmother's handkerchief (the only keepsake this woman had left from her grandmother) – so that her granddaughter would remember them all.

Bestow Your Furniture

A line that's repeated in *Something to Remember Me By* is: "Someday, that cedar chest at the foot of the bed will be yours." My grandmother picked out a piece of furniture to give each of her children and grandchildren. From the time I was five years old, I knew the cedar chest was mine. And I took care of it! Her other pieces of furniture were subject to the bumps and scratches that children inevitably inflict on furniture, but I was always careful around the cedar chest. Today it sits proudly at the foot of my bed.

Assign a special piece of furniture to each of your grandchildren (and children). It's like giving twice, now and in the future. It makes your grandchildren feel special and important, creates a bond, and helps build a sense of responsibility.

Tell the Story

When you give a keepsake, particularly an item with a family history to it, make sure you share the story behind it. Write down the story in a note when you pass along the keepsake. Is it a ring your father gave to your mother? A quilt your great-grandmother made? Why is the item important? Where did it come from?

Stories are what bring objects alive. That's the real power of a keepsake – not necessarily what it is, but what it means in the context of your life story.

When you share a keepsake's story, often even young children can understand its meaning at some level. There was one precocious little girl who told me, "My grandma gave my mom a very beautiful ring, and someday she's going to give it to me, and someday I'll give it to my daughter. That's the way you make history."

Family Tree

Help your grandchildren understand their place in the larger context of their family. Doing a simple family tree together can be an extended project with older grandchildren. It also becomes a keepsake.

You and your grandchildren can make a diagram of your family tree, perhaps including photographs. There is computer software available for charting family trees. Or, get a large sheet of paper and some pencil crayons or markers. Show your grandchildren where to draw boxes for various relatives, starting at the bottom with the oldest generation you know about and then branching out. You might want to use one color for one side of the family and a different color for the other.

Depending on how much you know and what research you do, you can also write a brief story about each family member under their photo.

Family Crest

Do you have a family crest? If not, you and your grandchildren can design one to be passed down to future generations.

Start by explaining that a crest or coat of arms is a special picture of your family (look in an encyclopedia to get some examples). Talk about the things that are a big part of your particular family's history, values, and interests. What symbols can you use to represent your family?

Then, cut out a shield or circle from stiff paper or cardboard. Have stencils, rulers, crayons, markers, and paint available. Be creative! You can experiment with several different designs until you develop one that everyone likes.

Once your crest is complete, hang it proudly. You can even photocopy it and make greeting cards to send notes to family members.

Family Book of Records

Your family, like many others, probably has amazing feats that should be recorded for posterity. Start a family book of records that can be passed around now for family fun and, over the long term, passed down to future generations.

Get a big, 3-ring binder. Use divider sheets to make categories: Sports; Toys and Games; Mathematics; Spelling; etc. Then put out various family challenges: What's the largest number of blocks your grandchildren can stack? What's the longest jump they can make? How long can they balance on one foot? Who is the family Scrabble or trivia champ? Who's the best at multiplication flash cards?

Write down the feat, date, record, record holder and their age. You can include a photograph or drawing if you have one. If you don't want to emphasize competition among grandchildren, each grandchild can compete against themselves (trying to better their own personal achievement). Another friendly rule: no one can challenge another person's record for at least a couple of days – so that everyone gets their moment of fame.

Family Time Capsule

You and your grandchildren, even if you live far away from each other, can collect items to put into a time capsule.

Collect personal items like family photos, school artwork, greeting cards, clothing, and family stories. You can also clip out current articles from magazines and newspapers, put in a hit CD, include clothing catalogs with the latest fashions, and make a list of popular movies, celebrities, and expressions. Put everything into a sealed storage container with the current date. Then, set a date five years or so into the future (long enough, but not too long) when your family will get together for a party to open the time capsule. Mark the container, "Do not open until…" Store it in a safe place. Now everyone has something to look forward to!

Keepsakes and Rituals

There are some things you do again and again over time that become family rituals. Rituals provide adults and children with something that is consistent, reliable, cherished, and predictable to look forward to. They become part of a family's identity. In this often hectic world, we could all use a few more rituals. If you don't have any family traditions or rituals, start some.

Rituals often become tied to keepsakes. For example, your grandchildren might enjoy the special holiday foods you cook year after year. Collect these recipes in a cookbook for posterity.

Perhaps each Christmas you can start a tradition of giving each of your grandchildren a special ornament. Or you and your grandchildren can have a ritual of pulling out the "special" playing cards or backgammon game for a family tournament. Or you can plan to attend the home opener every year of a local sports team and collect the programs.

If you have a regular family reunion, each time get T-shirts made for everyone with your family name, and maybe a familiar family saying.

Keepsakes and rituals become the things your grandchildren carry on into their families, often with the words, "I remember when Grandma..." A part of you will always remain in their lives.

"There are two people you have to be true to – those people who came before you and those people who came after you."

Gayl Jones

The 5 Life Lessons of Grandparenthood

THERE'S AN OLD SAYING that grandparenthood is nature's reward for aging. Not only is it a reward in itself, but it's an opportunity for additional rewards. It's a chance to learn some very fundamental life lessons. It's a chance to learn about yourself and grow as a person, and to participate in the growth of others, particularly your grandchildren and adult children. It's a chance to make a difference and leave an important legacy.

Grandparenthood offers five key life lessons:

Life Lesson #1: Grandparenting is Different Than Parenting

Life Lesson #2: The Legacy You Leave is as Strong as The Love You Give

Life Lesson #3: We Are All Part of a Bigger Life Connection

Life Lesson #4: Memories Are The Stories of Our Lives

Life Lesson #5: Building a Loving Connection is a Process

Life Lesson #1: Grandparenting is Different Than Parenting

As the joke goes, "If I had known how much fun being a grand-parent is, I would have done it first."

The parent/child relationship is one of the most important and complex relationships we have in our lives. On the other hand, the grandparent/grandchild relationship is one of the most magical. Grandparenting is very different from parenting. So many people say they feel a "joyful freedom" in their role as grandparents. And just as many value the "second chance" grandparenthood gives them. Grandchildren are a fresh start. The kind of unconditional love grandparents and grandchildren experience can be even more powerful than romantic love.

As a grandparent, you have to understand the difference between the love of a parent and the love of a grandparent – and celebrate it. Don't take the relationship for granted. A parent's job is to raise children to be responsible, independent people in the future. Your job as a grandparent is basically to love children for who they are in the moment. In the time of miniskirts, while one teenager's mother worried about her morals, the grandmother helped her granddaughter raise the hem on all her skirts. Today, that woman has turned out just fine – thanks to the combination of the love of both her mother and grandmother.

There are some grandparents today who do have to raise their grandchildren because, for a variety of reasons, the parents are unable to. In fact, there are millions of such grandparents. As far as I'm concerned, these grandparents are heroes. They often keep families together which would otherwise be torn apart. When I've spoken to these grandparents, they say that raising their grandchildren can be time-consuming, costly, and draining, with little social or legal support. But they also admit it has rewards. It can give them a new lease on life, and make them feel wanted at a time in their lives when society may not value them anymore. And although they must in part fulfill the role of parent, they don't lose all of their grandparent magic. Children know their grandparents have chosen to create a safe, loving home for them, and so the grandparents have a very special place in their grand-children's hearts.

What any grandparent sees in the face of their grandchild is joy and hope. As someone who has lived on this earth for many years, you have hopefully gained some insight and wisdom. Combining the hope of the young with the wisdom of older adults is what effective living is all about. It may *seem* as though children are growing up faster today. But in many ways they are more overwhelmed and more underprepared. They are exposed to more things, and they may be more sophisticated, but they are not really mature. They need the guidance and love of a grandparent. They need you.

Life Lesson #2: The Legacy You Leave is as Strong as The Love You Give

We all want to be remembered. We all want to feel as though we've made a difference in this world.

Psychologists have found there are four universal human needs found in all nations, races, religions, and cultures: 1) the need to live; 2) the need to learn; 3) the need to love; and 4) the need to leave a legacy. For most of us, the need to leave a legacy is at least in part tied to the need to love. We need to feel as though we've made a difference in the lives of the people we love, particularly our children and grandchildren.

Leaving a legacy for those we love has a selfish component to it: we want to feel immortal. By connecting with those at the beginning of their lives, we complete a full circle in life's journey and leave some of our "selves" – our experiences, ideas, values, and personal example – in the minds and hearts of others. Making a difference in the lives of our children and grandchildren also has an altruistic component. If we don't leave a legacy of love, what kind of society are we building, what kind of world are we leaving behind?

You can be a role model for your grandchildren, and make

them and the world better. You can model good behavior, values, and ethics. Don't just talk it, walk it! You will also become a better person for yourself.

Whenever I talk about legacies, the topic of death inevitably comes up. Have you ever tried the "funeral exercise"? In your mind, see yourself going to the funeral of a loved one. Picture yourself driving to the funeral home, parking the car, and getting out. As you walk into the building, you notice the flowers, cards, and soft organ music. You see the faces of friends and family as you walk into the room. You feel the shared sense of loss. As you walk to the front of the room and look inside the casket, you suddenly come face-to-face with yourself. This is your funeral, at some time in the distant future. As you sit down for the service, your grandchild rises to speak. What would you like them to say about you? What will they remember about you? What difference will you have made in their life? What legacy do you want to leave?

We don't like to think about death. But death is what makes life precious. Because grandparenthood is one of life's major transitions, it is an opportunity to reevaluate some fundamental life questions before it's too late: What have I done with my life? What is worth doing now? How can I still make the world a better place? If you focus on your regrets and give up hope, then you can't share yourself with your grandchildren and adult children, and there is no hope. You can make another choice.

We live in a youth-obsessed culture, so it's hard to grow old gracefully and with wisdom. We send children a contradictory message – we want them to respect their elders, and yet we work desperately to look anything but. In a society that doesn't want to acknowledge aging, let alone death, the grandparent/grandchild relationship is also your opportunity to explore the cycle of life for yourself and your grandchildren.

You may still be vital and healthy, and have many good years ahead. But if you are lucky to live long enough, that will change. You are a living example of growing old. Aging is as natural as the changing seasons. It says that you've lived and learned.

Try doing something as simple as comparing your hands with your young grandchild's. You'll be surprised to discover that grandchildren often want their hands to look like yours! Children don't fear aging until we teach them to. Perhaps you can learn a little something from your grandchildren. How you face your own aging and illnesses will in turn be a lesson to your grandchildren on how to view their own life. You and your grandchildren can learn from each other.

Children today have more indirect contact with death through television and movies, but less direct, real contact. Further, television and movies rarely depict the prolonged reality of pain, tears, and grief. How can children learn to deal with these life realities? How you talk to your grandchildren about death and prepare them for it is important, particularly if you have built a close connection and losing you will be a significant life loss for them. Most children aged five and up need to say good-bye to a grandparent if they are ill or dying, and they need help dealing with their feelings. Facing the mortality of those before us is the only way we can understand our own mortality.

Talk to your grandchildren about death – not in a morbid way, but in a matter-of-fact way. Be calm and open, without overloading them. If you're willing to talk about the hard stuff, kids are willing too. If you're grieving the loss of a friend or relative, it's okay to let your grandchildren see some of your pain. Sharing your feelings builds closeness. Part of your legacy of love is to help your grandchildren know about dying, as well as living.

Always remember that a legacy of love is as much about the present as it is about the future. I love the comic strip at the start of this book: a proud granddaughter brings her grandmother to school as her most precious treasure. That's what the grandma connection is all about. It's clear that the grandma in the comic strip has created a legacy of love. I was surprised recently to hear a real-life story that mirrors the comic strip.

A teacher read *Something to Remember Me By* to her class. She and her students had a big discussion about the story, keepsakes, and grandparents. The teacher then asked each of the children to bring in something that was special to them and tell the class about it. One girl asked if she could bring in her grandmother. A visit with grandma was organized. Grandma brought in a craft activity and the whole class participated. After the visit, the children all wrote "thank you" notes to the grandmother. The teacher said it was some of the best writing she had ever seen her students do. Grandma responded with a note of her own, and gingerbread cookies. This grandmother has created a living legacy of love for her granddaughter, and for every child in that class.

Life Lesson #3: We Are All Part of a Bigger Life Connection

More than 2,000 years ago, the Greek philosopher Heraclitus expressed the connectedness of all things:

> Out of life comes death, and out of death, life. Out of the young, the old and out of the old, the young. Out of waking, sleep, and out of sleep, waking. The stream of creation and dissolution never stops.

There is an unstoppable flow to life, as one generation melts into the next. Relationships between young and old, between grandparents and grandchildren, make us feel connected. They make us feel connected not only to each other, but to something bigger, to the past and to the future, to a basic life force. In this hectic, high-tech world, we need this sense of connection. In fact, we crave it. It helps us understand who we are, where we've come from, where we're going, and why we're going there. In connection there is meaning, purpose, and joy.

For your grandchildren, the grandma connection is about having a sense of "we" as well as "I." It's a link to a world of the past your grandchildren can never know directly, and to a world of the future they must be prepared for. Your grandchildren also learn from you what being loved is all about and how to love someone.

For you, the grandma connection isn't just about connecting with your grandchildren. It's about *reconnecting* with what really matters in life, with the life force within you. Active, involved grandparents live longer, healthier lives. They consistently report less depression and higher degrees of life satisfaction and happiness.

Grandparenthood is a reminder of time passed and time passing. For some, grandchildren may come along at a time when your life force might be beginning to fade – years of disappointment, of unfilled expectations and dreams, heartache, changes, and challenges. You've come a long way. You've raised children, with all the pride and fears that brings with it. You've done the best job you could. You've made mistakes. You've made good decisions. You now have the benefit of hindsight – which is, of course, another word for wisdom. And through wisdom comes maturity. Maturity is about acknowledging everything that has happened in your life and facing it with integrity, honesty, and goodness. It's about accepting responsibility for your life, your choices, and your happiness.

"Mature" doesn't mean you're finished though. We're never "all grown up." The life cycle goes on, with each stage presenting its own challenges and opportunities to grow. That's where your grandchildren come in. By staying in touch with younger generations, you grow and live your life to the fullest.

Grandchildren have the power to rekindle your life force if it's fading. Research shows that something as simple as playing tapes of grandchildren in nursing homes gives even very ill residents a physical and psychological boost. A woman I know went into a very deep depression after the death of her husband of 56 years. The only thing that got her out of her depression was a two-year-old girl. The little girl was a neighbor and, when she was out playing one day with her mother, unexpectedly ran over to the woman and gave her a big grin. Over time, the little girl became the woman's "adopted grandchild," and helped her rekindle her reason for living.

Grandchildren shouldn't become your whole life, but they can help you put things in perspective. While you want to help your grandchildren understand the realities of aging by, for example, sharing your feelings about a health problem you have developed, you don't want to dwell on your problems. By taking delight in and focussing on hearing about *your grandchildren's* lives, you help them and yourself.

Grandchildren make you smile and laugh. They make your life less sterile and stagnant, and more real. They make you proud. They make you believe in life's possibilities. They help you remember – the things you said you'd do, the things you hoped you'd do. They give you an excuse to shop. They energize you – pushing you to crawl around on the floor when you could hardly imagine it. They prevent you from taking life, and yourself, too seriously. And don't forget that grandmothers are attracted to other grandmothers, and inevitably start swapping stories. That's also a part of the grandma connection that brings energy into your life.

Ultimately, the connection between grandparents and grandchildren has a give-and-take to it that is life giving to both generations. Older people can give much to the young, and the young can give back much to older people. At the beginning of *Something to Remember Me By*, it's the grandmother who gives to her young granddaughter – all her love, time, and attention. She builds a loving grandma connection, just as my grandmother built a loving connection with me. Toward the end of the story, the grandmother is very, very old. The grown granddaughter then gives back to her grandmother. She helps her grandmother move. She gives her grandmother comfort and support. She holds her grandmother's hand when she needs it most. She gives back out of love.

At the end of the story, the flow of life is symbolized by the grandmother's cedar chest sitting at the foot of the grown granddaughter's bed. The granddaughter realizes that the most precious gift her grandmother gave her was her love – and the happy memories it created. There is also a sense of the continuity in life. The final image of the smiling granddaughter symbolizes much more than a physical similarity to her grandmother. The granddaughter has her grandmother's "big, warm smile," meaning that who her grandmother was – loving, warm, full of life – has, in part, made the granddaughter who she is. The grandmother will always be with her granddaughter. The grandmother and granddaughter are both part of a much bigger life connection.

Life Lesson #4: Memories Are The Stories of Our Lives

It seems to me that if you're going to explore relationships across generations, you need a story that reaches both children and adults. That's why I wrote *Something to Remember Me By* – a book inspired by my own memories of my grandmother – for both adults and children. It reaches all ages, but differently. For adults, it evokes memories and emotions. For children, it's a snuggly story, and also the kind of story you can use to discuss important life issues.

After I read *Something to Remember Me By* out loud in my mixed workshops with grandparents and grandchildren, I encourage everyone to talk about how they feel about the story and ask questions. The conversations can get pretty amazing. Once, a little girl asked, "What's a memory?" An older gentleman in the group answered by saying, "It's something warm in your heart." Then everyone, young and old, started talking about what made their heart warm.

A woman in Kansas City wanted me to sign a copy of *Something to Remember Me By* to her 81-year-old mother, who's in a nursing home. The woman said she visits her mom every few days, and runs out of things to talk about. She took the book with her one day and read it to her mom as a way to pass the time. She said they both had a good cry after reading the story – and then the best talk. They talked about family memories, about all kinds of things they hadn't talked about in years. It was the kind of talk you know you should have, but somehow never get around to having.

Memories are the story of our life that exists in our mind. They help us make sense of our life and find meaning in it. They can be very powerful. Even today, when I'm going through a rough time, it's the memory of my grandmother and how she was always in my corner that gives me strength. Memories give us comfort, hope, inspiration, and direction.

Modern education favors lists, labels, theories and numbers more than information shared through story. Because of this, many people don't see a story in their lives anymore. They see a string of events occurring around them and to them, but they don't necessarily put these events together into a life story that carries important meaning for them.

Poet, writer, and activist Muriel Rukeyser once said, "The universe is made of stories, not of atoms." Communication scholar W. Barnett Pearce puts it this way:

Human beings are confronted with certain "facts of life." We are born, we mature, and then we die. While alive, we eat, excrete, and interact with our fellows. And we invest all of these "facts" with meaning by placing them within stories. Making "meaning" is not an optional activity in which persons sometimes engage; it is part of what it means to be a human being.

The quality of your memories, of the mental story you tell yourself, affects the quality of the life you create. Celebrate your memories. Treasure them. Think about what makes your "heart warm." This will help you create good things in your life. And then, create good memories for your grandchildren. When you consciously create loving memories for your grandchildren, you create a loving life story for yourself and for them.

Make the most of the moments today that will be tomorrow's memories. They will become a part of your grandchildren's life story, and they will build a connection that transcends time.

Life Lesson #5: Building a Loving Connection is a Process

You're now a grandparent full of life wisdom! I don't have to tell you that ultimately happiness is all about the positive emotional relationships you consciously and consistently work at building with those who are important to you.

Building a loving grandparent connection is a work in progress. There is no end. You can always make it better, always add a bit here or there.

As I said at the start, there's no magic to building the grandparent connection. It can *be* a magical relationship, but you need no magic to get there. I've reminded you what it's all about, and given you some guidelines on how to put all the pieces together. The rest is up to you.

I am more convinced than ever that the more complicated life gets, the more the simple things count. Remember that line in *Something to Remember Me By*: "She gave her a big, warm smile and a warm, snuggly hug." That's the essence of the grandparent connection. That's what we all need – whether you're a child or a grown-up. It's that simple. Do you know that research shows that the older people get, the fewer hugs we give them? We give teenagers fewer hugs than toddlers, and 70-year-olds fewer hugs than 20-year-olds. Your goal is to give lots of hugs. And I hope that, in turn, your grandchildren will come to give you lots of hugs.

The process of grandparenthood inevitably starts with the simple, little things. It's the little things that make you fall in love with your grandchild – like holding them for the first time, feeling their little hand curl around your finger, seeing a smile bubble up on their face. The intensity and depth of this love often comes as a surprise to grandparents. After that, your every little facial expression, every tiny gesture, every seemingly small action, every word of even one syllable, is making the connection between you and your grandchild.

It is all part of the process.

When your "baby" has a baby, you search for the right balance between comfortable old habits and new experiences. You feel, think, and plan your way into your new role. Traditions may change as a new family is born. When people become parents, there are usually two sets of grandparents – and two sets of traditions and backgrounds – to deal with. Things change, your connection with your children changes.

It is all part of the process.

Recognize that being a grandparent isn't necessarily a full-time job. Live your life in balance. Give your new role no less and no more attention than it deserves. Celebrate who you are and where you are in your life. Know that you will make mistakes. Know that you will do some things better than you thought you could. Know that there will be moments of frustration balanced by moments of tremendous joy. This is an opportunity to reconnect with yourself and what's important in life.

It is all part of the process.

The new relationships with your grandchildren and adult children give you a chance to learn and grow. Be willing to keep learning. Pay attention to everything, to all the little things. The more aware you are, the more you will find meaning and joy. Be willing to put listening ahead of talking. Remember that when you listen and give someone – adult or child – your understanding and support, you help them and you help your relationship. Enjoy visits; spend time in the kitchen; lose yourself in the fun of play; make use of photographs and letter writing; share stories; give gifts and keepsakes. Keep your heart open to all the new connections in your life.

It is all part of the process.

And the ultimate result of this process? Children can grow to accomplish great things in this world when they know that someone believes in them. You can be that someone in your grandchild's life. And you will be the best grandparent, parent, and person you can be.

Great Books & Resources

Books to Share with Your Grandchildren

*"If you see a book, a rocking chair, and a grandchild
in the same room, don't pass up a chance to
read aloud. Instill in your grandchildren a love
of reading. It's one of the greatest gifts you can give."*

Barbara Bush

Children learn to love reading when adults around them love it. Sharing a love of reading with your grandchildren is truly one of the most natural and best intergenerational gifts you can give. It also helps your grandchildren develop important communication skills (i.e. reading, writing, listening, talking). Some tips:

- Surround your grandchildren with books of all kinds. Have them in your home, and give them as gifts.

- Take your grandchildren on frequent trips to the library and the bookstore.

- Let your grandchildren choose their own books, but also encourage them to try books they might not normally choose.

- Start your own family book club – give or send your grandchildren a new book each month.

- During visits, grandparents are in an ideal position to cuddle up and spend time reading to grandchildren. Read aloud – even with older grandchildren. And talk about what you've read. For the rest of their lives, your grandchildren will associate the pleasure and intimacy of the experience with each book they read.

Here are some great picture books (you're never "too old" to enjoy the beauty and message of a picture book!) that you can share with your grandchildren. Many are about special relationships across generations; others are just good reads. You can also share stories you enjoyed when you were young, or that your children enjoyed. For more recommended books, visit the Legacy Project at www.legacyproject.org.

Aliki. *Communication.* Greenwillow Books, 1993. A wonderful book that explores all the ways and all the feelings and ideas that people communicate.

Aliki. *The Two of Them.* Greenwillow Books, 1979. The story of a grandfather's relationship with his granddaughter, from her birth to his death.

Anholt, Laurence and Dan Williams illus. *The Magpie Song*. Houghton Mifflin, 1996. Carla, who lives with her family in the city, shares a close relationship – and a secret – with her grandad in the country through the letters they write each other.

Atwell, Debby. *Pearl*. Houghton Mifflin, 2001. Beginning with the time her grandfather was scooped out of a crowd to ride alongside George Washington in his Inauguration Day parade, 98-year-old Pearl tells the fascinating story of her life, which intersects with many significant historical events and people.

Bang, Molly. *The Grey Lady and the Strawberry Snatcher*. Simon & Schuster, 1980. In this detailed, wordless story, an eerie strawberry snatcher tries to snatch strawberries from a woman cloaked all in grey.

Bogart, Jo Ellen and Barbara Reid illus. *Gifts*. North Winds Press, 1994. With delightful verse, a grandma brings her granddaughter souvenirs from her travels throughout the world.

Bosak, Susan V. with 15 top illustrators in the world. *Dream: A Tale of Wonder, Wisdom & Wishes*. TCP Press, 2004. This inspiring celebration of hopes and dreams across a lifetime combines gorgeous illustrations with a beautifully told poetic story. It's a special gift grandparents can give a new grandchild, and a book they can share with older grandchildren to help them become aware of their own dreams and goals.

Bosak, Susan V. and Laurie McGaw illus. *Something to Remember Me By*. The Communication Project, 1997, 2003. In this moving story, a grandmother gives her young granddaughter special keepsakes; as the years pass and both grow older, it becomes clear the love they share is the most precious gift of all.

Bowen, Anne and Greg Shed illus. *I Loved You Before You Were Born*. Harpercollins, 2001. A sweet story about a grandmother eagerly awaiting the arrival of her grandchild; when the baby finally arrives, Grandma is ready with a special message.

Buckley, Helen E. and Jan Ormerod illus. *Grandfather and I* and *Grandmother and I*. Lothrop, Lee, and Shepard, 1994. Two warm, reassuring companion books, told from the perspective of a child.

Carle, Eric. *Draw Me a Star*. Penguin Putnam, 1998. A multilayered celebration of imagination, a young artist creates a world of light and possibility.

Christian, Frank P., Wendy Gelsanliter and Marjorie Priceman illus. *Dancin' in the Kitchen*. Putnam, 1998. While making dinner at Grandma's, all three generations of a family have a great time dancing to the music on the kitchen radio.

Combs, Ann. *How Old is Old?* Price Stern Sloan, 1988. Alistair isn't sure how old "old" really is until his grandfather shows him, in charming rhyme, that everything is relative.

Cooney, Barbara. *Miss Rumphius*. Viking, 1985. A lovely, inspiring book about an older woman who, as a young girl, vows to see faraway places, live beside the sea, and do something to make the world more beautiful. She does all of these things, with the last one being most important of all.

Cronin, Doreen and Betsy Lewin illus. *Click, Clack, Moo: Cows That Type*. Simon & Schuster, 2000. When the cows find a typewriter, the plucky barnyard animals unite to improve their conditions.

Crystal, Billy and Elizabeth Sayles illus. *I Already Know I Love You.* HarperCollins, 2004. Beginning with anticipating a new baby's arrival, this heartfelt book celebrates all the moments – great and small – that a new grandpa is ready to share.

DiTerlizzi, Tony. *The Spider and the Fly.* Simon & Schuster, 2002. Silver-sheened black-and-white illustrations complement this clever retelling of a classic story.

Dorros, Arthur and Elisa Kleven illus. *Abuela.* Puffin, 1997. Rosalba and her grandmother, her abuela, take a magical journey as they fly over the streets of Manhattan. The story is narrated in English sprinkled with Spanish phrases.

English, Karen and Cedric Lucas illus. *Big Wind Coming!* Albert Whitman, 1996. An African-American family gets through a hurricane on their farm with the help of their grandparents' quiet wisdom.

Fox, Mem and Patricia Mullins illus. *Shoes from Grandpa.* Orchard Books, 1992. In a playful cumulative rhyme, family members describe the clothes they intend to give Jessie to go with her shoes from Grandpa.

Fox, Mem and Julie Vivas illus. *Wilfrid Gordon McDonald Partridge.* Viking Kestrel, 1984. A young boy learns what memory is and helps an old woman remember times from her life.

Franklin, Kristine L. and Terea Shaffer illus. *The Old, Old Man and the Very Little Boy.* Atheneum, 1992. In an African village, an ancient storyteller passes on wonderful tales to a little boy who, one day, will carry on the storytelling tradition.

Garza, Carmen Lomas. *Family Pictures/Cuadros de familia.* Childrens Book Press, 1993. A bilingual memoir of one family's life – all ages and generations – in Texas near the Mexican border.

Gilman, Phoebe. *Something from Nothing.* Scholastic, 1992. From a Jewish folktale, this charming story begins as Joseph's mother wants to throw away his tattered, beloved blanket. But Grandpa will fix it!

Hawxhurst, Joan C. and Jane K. Bynum illus. *Bubbe & Gram.* Dovetail Publishing, 1996. A child learns about Christianity and Judaism from her two very different grandmothers.

Heal, Gillian. *Grandpa Bear's Fantastic Scarf.* Beyond Words Publishing, 1997. Each day, Grandpa Bear's weaving grows longer and more colorful, reflecting pieces of his life.

Hest, Amy and Amy Schwartz illus. *The Purple Coat.* Four Winds Press, 1986. Mama wants her to get a practical navy blue coat, but Gabby's grampa understands why Gabby wants a purple coat.

Hoffman, Mary and Caroline Binch illus. *Amazing Grace.* Dial, 1991. Nana helps her African-American granddaughter Grace understand that she can be anything, "if you put your mind to it."

Johnson, Angela and David Soman illus. *When I Am Old With You.* Orchard, 1993. An affectionate tale of an African-American child who looks forward to getting old and doing the same things with his grandfather that he does now.

Johnson, Tony and Harvey Stevenson illus. *Little Rabbit Goes to Sleep.* HarperCollins, 1994. Grandpa helps little bunny understand the night in this delightful story for helping little ones sleep.

Keens-Douglas, Richardo and Frances Clancy illus. *Grandpa's Visit.* Annick Press, 1996. Grandpa visits from the Caribbean; Jeremy is busy with TV and video games until Grandpa gives the family a simple gift.

Keller, Holly. *Grandfather's Dream.* Greenwillow, 1994. A small boy shares his grandfather's dream of helping the cranes, a symbol of good luck, return to their Vietnam village.

Kesselman, Wendy and Barbara Cooney illus. *Emma.* Picture Yearling, 1993. On Emma's 72nd birthday her four children, seven grandchildren, and fourteen great-grandchildren give her a painting that prompts her to begin to paint and opens a whole new life for her.

Kindersley, Barnabas and Anabel. *Children Just Like Me.* DK Publishing, 1995. Published for UNICEF's 50th anniversary, share the lives, hopes, and dreams of children from around the world.

Koralek, Jenny and James Mayhew illus. *The Boy and the Cloth of Dreams.* Candlewick, 1996. A lyrical tale about a special quilt made by grandma that helps a boy overcome his fears.

Lindbergh, Reeve and R. Isadora illus. *Grandfather's Lovesong.* Viking, 1993. A poetic description of a grandfather's love for his grandson, using nature metaphors through the seasons.

Lindbergh, Reeve and Stephen Lambert illus. *What Is The Sun?* Candlewick, 1994. In delightful rhyming text, a grandmother answers all of her grandson's questions about the world as he gets ready for bed.

MacLachlan, Patricia and Deborah Ray illus. *Through Grandpa's Eyes.* Harper & Row, 1980. John learns a rich and detailed way of seeing the world from his blind grandfather.

Marcellino, Fred. *I, Crocodile*. HarperCollins, 1999. A delightful, witty alligator describes his travels from being an idol in Egypt to a captive curiosity in Napoleon's France.

Marsden, John. *Prayer for the Twenty-First Century*. Star Bright Books, 1998. Brilliantly illustrated with paintings, photos, and collages, this compelling call from the heart contains a message of hope that is a legacy we would wish for all our loved ones.

McCain, Becky Ray and Stacey Schuett illus. *Grandmother's Dreamcatcher*. Albert Whitman, 1998. When Kimmy has bad dreams, Grandmother shows her how to make a dreamcatcher. Includes instructions for making a dreamcatcher.

McFarlane, Sheryl and Ron Lightburn illus. *Waiting for the Whales*. Orca, 1991. An old man has only the whales in the nearby ocean to keep him company until his young granddaughter gives him a renewed purpose in life.

McPhail, David. *Mole Music*. Henry Holt, 1999. In this tenderhearted tale, Mole learns to make beautiful, joyful music that has the power to change the world.

Mellonie, Bryan and Robert Ingpen illus. *Beginnings and Endings with Lifetimes in Between*. Paper Tiger, 1983. A beautiful, moving book that explains the cycle of life.

Millard, Anne and Steve Noon illus. *A Street Through Time*. DK Publishing, 1998. Have you ever wondered what your street was like 100 years ago? This fascinating book traces the development of one street from the Stone Age through 14 time periods to the present day, including information about how people lived.

Murdoch, Patricia and Kellie Jobson illus. *Deep Thinker And The Stars.* Three Trees Press, 1987. A gentle story reflecting the cultures of native peoples, Deep Thinker remembers her grandfather when her new baby brother arrives.

Numeroff, Laura Joffe and Lynn Munsinger illus. *What Grandmas Do Best, What Grandpas Do Best.* Simon & Schuster, 2000. Read one way this book celebrates the joyful relationship between children and their grandmas, and read the other way it's about the fun children have with their grandpas.

Oberman, Sheldon and Ted Lewin illus. *The Always Prayer Shawl.* Boyds Mills Press, 1994. A prayer shawl is handed down from grandfather to grandson in a story of Jewish tradition and the passing of generations.

Opie, Iona (ed) and Rosemary Wells illus. *My Very First Mother Goose.* Candlewick, 1996. A collection of more than 60 classic rhymes with playful illustrations.

Paul, Ann Whitford and Maggie Smith illus. *Everything to Spend the Night from A to Z.* DK Publishing, 1999. A humorous tale about a girl who goes to visit her grandfather and packs items representing every letter in the alphabet.

Polacco, Patricia. *The Keeping Quilt.* Simon & Schuster, 1998. A homemade quilt ties together the lives of four generations of a Jewish family.

Puttock, Simon and Alison Jay illus. *A Ladder to the Stars.* Henry Holt, 2001. A little girl sees a dancing star and makes a wish, only to climb a ladder to that star when she is an old woman.

Rattigan, Jama Kim and Lillian Hsu-Flanders illus. *Dumpling Soup*. Little, Brown, 1998. Marisa gets to join in making dumpling soup with all the other women in the family and gets some special encouragement from grandma.

Reid, Barbara. *The Party*. Scholastic, 1999. A delightful tale, with unique plasticine illustrations, about all the family fun at Grandma's birthday party.

Rochelle, Belinda, and Cornelius Van Wright and Ying-Hwa Hu illus. *Jewels*. Lodestar, 1998. The "jewels" of the title are family stories of African-American history Lea Mae hears on her summer vacation with her great-grandparents.

Rylant, Cynthia and Kathryn Brown illus. *The Old Woman Who Named Things*. Voyager, 2000. A feisty old woman who has outlived all her friends starts naming only things that will outlive her, until a homeless pup enters the scene.

Scheffler, Ursel and Ruth Scholte Van Mast illus. *Grandpa's Amazing Computer*. North South Books, 1997. When Ollie visits his grandfather, he discovers that although the man doesn't have a clue about Ollie's computer, he has an amazing computer of his own.

Schulman, Janet (ed). *The 20th Century Children's Book Treasury*. Alfred A. Knopf, 1998. This collection of 44 read-aloud classics from *Goodnight Moon* to *Stellaluna* is perfect for sharing with young grandchildren.

Schulman, Janet (ed). *You Read to Me & I'll Read to You: 20th Century Stories to Share*. Alfred A. Knopf, 2001. If your grandchildren are too old for the collection above, this treasury offers you much to share together (because you're never "too old" to be read to!). 26 read-aloud classics from *The Piggy in the Puddle* to *Cloudy with a Chance of Meatballs*.

Schwartz, David M. and Bert Dodson illus. *Supergrandpa*. Lothrop, Lee & Shepard, 1991. The true story of a 66-year-old cyclist who rode in the tour of Sweden – against everyone's advice! – and challenged all the stereotypes.

Seuss, Dr. and Steve Johnson and Lou Fancher illus. *My Many Colored Days*. Alfred A. Knopf, 1996. A rhyming story that describes each day in terms of a particular color which is in turn associated with a certain emotion. A book that appeals to all ages and is great for prompting discussion about emotions.

Shannon, George and David Soman illus. *This Is the Bird*. Houghton Mifflin, 1997. A cumulative tale about a wooden bird carved by a girl's maternal ancestor and lovingly passed down from mother to daughter through the generations.

Shaw, Eve. *Grandmother's Alphabet*. Scholastic, 2001. The message of this empowering alphabet book is simple: Grandma can be a zoologist, artist, banker, carpenter, doctor, engineer... and so can I.

Shulevitz, Uri. *Dawn*. Farrar, Straus and Giroux, 1974. Inspired by a Chinese poem, this beautiful book tells of an old man and his grandson sharing the beauty of daybreak.

Spedden, Daisy Corning Stone and Laurie McGaw illus. *Polar The Titanic Bear*. Little, Brown, 1994. The true story of a toy bear named Polar and a little boy who survive the sinking of the Titanic. Includes historical background information and photographs throughout.

Steig, William and Teryl Euvremer illus. *Toby, Where Are You?* HarperCollins, 1997. In this classic interactive book for very young children, Toby, a mischievous small animal, has lots of fun hiding from his parents.

Ul de Rico. *The Rainbow Goblins*. Thames & Hudson, 2001. This classic tale about imagination brings together fantastic colors, amazing detail, and a sweeping scope.

Walsh, Jill Paton and Stephen Lambert illus. *When I Was Little Like You*. Viking, 1997. Simple now-and-then comparisons as Rosie and Gran go for a stroll are ideal for sharing and inviting children to question their own grandparents.

Ward, Helen and Wayne Anderson illus. *The Tin Forest*. Dutton, 2001. A lovely fable about imagination and creativity, a man creates a beautiful forest from a seemingly forlorn environment.

Wayland, April Halprin and George Booth illus. *It's Not My Turn To Look for Grandma!* Knopf, 1995. A farm family takes turns keeping track of their mischievous grandmother, who joins in with the farm animals in a riotous display of joke telling, haystack sliding, card shuffling, and banjo playing.

Weate, Jeremy (ed) and Peter Lawman illus. *A Young Person's Guide to Philosophy*. DK Publishing, 1998. Introduces over 25 of the world's greatest philosophers in a fascinating, easy-to-understand style.

Weiss, George David, Bob Thiele, and Ashley Bryan illus. *What a Wonderful World*. Sundance, 1994. Inspired by Louis Armstrong's wonderful old song, this book is a great way to share a timeless message that can bring young and old together.

Wheeler, Lisa and Frank Ansley illus. *Wool Gathering: A Sheep Family Reunion*. Atheneum, 2001. This delightfully wooly tale about a family reunion celebrates all the different characters that make up any family.

Wiesner, David. *The Three Pigs*. Clarion, 2001. If you think you know this story, think again!

Wild, Margaret and Ron Brooks illus. *Old Pig*. Dial, 1996. Old Pig and Granddaughter have lived together for a long time, and they take one last, long walk together to savor the beauty of life around them.

Wild, Margaret and Julie Vivas illus. *Our Granny*. Houghton Mifflin, 1998. From the intimacy of one family to the rich diversity of all kinds of people, this exuberant book, told from the perspective of a small child, celebrates grandmothers.

Wood, Audrey and Don Wood Illus. *The Napping House*. Harcourt Brace, 1984. A delightful cumulative tale that all starts with a snoring granny. It's just plain fun!

Wood, Douglas and Cheng-Khee Chee illus. *Old Turtle*. Scholastic, 2001. An enchanting and beautiful fable about ecology, peace, and the interconnectedness of all things.

Wyse, Lois, Molly Rose Goldman and Marie-Louise Gay illus. *How to Take Your Grandmother to the Museum*. Workman, 1998. Written by a real grandmother and her ten-year-old granddaughter, this is a story about an adventurous girl, her willing grandmother, and the things they discover together in a museum.

Books & Resources for Grandparents

Here are some of the best books, organizations, and websites related to grandparenting and family. For more recommendations, visit the Legacy Project at www.legacyproject.org.

AARP. 601 E Street NW, Washington, DC 20049, (202) 434-2277 or (888) 687-2277, www.aarp.org. The largest organization for people age 50 and older. It offers resources, membership benefits, publications, and a Grandparent Information Center.

Bosak, Susan V. *Science Is…: A Source Book of Fascinating Facts, Projects and Activities*. Scholastic, 1991, 2000. Science is an educational, fun adventure grandparents and grandchildren can share. This classic has over 450 easy-to-do activities, projects, games, puzzles, and stories. Visit www.bigsciencebook.com.

Brown, Conrad Veazey. *Handbook for Grandfathers: How to Be a Pal to Your Grandchildren*. Writer's Showcase Press, 2000. A useful book that includes places to take grandchildren, gift ideas, and ways to keep in touch with long-distance grandkids.

Carson, Lillian. *The Essential Grandparent: A Guide to Making a Difference*. Health Communications, 1996. A wonderfully practical, warm, and intelligent book on modern grandparenting.

Carson, Lillian. *The Essential Grandparent's Guide to Divorce: Making a Difference in the Family*. Health Communications, 1999. An excellent guide on how to remain an effective parent and grandparent in situations of divorce and blended families.

Covey, Stephen. *The 7 Habits of Highly Effective Families*. Golden Books, 1997. With practical wisdom, Covey discusses principles for a strong, loving family that lasts for generations.

de Toledo, Sylvie and Deborah Edler Brown. *Grandparents as Parents*. Guilford Press, 1995. A realistic guide for grandparents raising grandchildren that includes information on handling troubled parents and their kids, dealing with drugs, lifestyle changes, custody issues, and other common concerns.

Edelman, Hope. *Mother of My Mother: The Intricate Bond Between Generations*. Dial, 1999. An evocative look at the relationships between grandmothers, mothers, and daughters.

Elderhostel. 11 Avenue de Lafayette, Boston, MA 02111-1746, (877) 426-8056 or (978) 323-4141, www.elderhostel.org. A non-profit organization that offers high-quality, affordable, educational adventures for adults 55 and older. They also offer unique intergenerational programs for grandparents and grandchildren.

Elgin, Suzette Haden. *The Grandmother Principles*. Abbeville Press, 1998. Practical and fun, this book suggests what not to do, and has ideas for building close bonds with grandchildren.

Experience Corps. 2120 L Street NW, Suite 400, Washington, DC 20037, (202) 478-6190, www.experiencecorps.org. Mobilizes the time, talent, and experience of older adults in service to the community, particularly mentoring programs in schools.

Floyd, Elaine. *Creating Family Newsletters*. F&W Publications, 1998. 123 ideas for sharing memorable moments with family.

Ford, Judy. *Wonderful Ways to Love a Grandchild*. Conari Press, 1997. Practical insights on being a modern grandparent.

Foundation for Grandparenting. 108 Farnham Rd, Ojai, CA 93023, www.grandparenting.org. Founded by grandparenting pioneer Arthur Kornhaber. It provides education, information, and networking.

Generations United. 1333 H Street NW, Suite 500 W, Washington, DC 20005, (202) 289-3979, www.gu.org. Promotes intergenerational strategies, programs, and policies. It is a coalition of over 100 organizations, and offers a number of publications and a newsletter.

Grandtravel. 1920 N Street NW, Suite 200, Washington, DC 20036-1601, (800) 247-7651 or (202) 785-8901, www.grandtrvl.com. A travel service for grandparents looking for fun vacation ideas with their grandkids.

Greene, Bob and D.G. Fulford. *To Our Children's Children: Preserving Family Histories for Generations to Come*. Doubleday, 1993. An accessible guide for creating written and oral histories.

Greer, Colin and Herbert Kohl (eds). *A Call to Character: A Family Treasury*. HarperCollins, 1995. A wonderful reader for grandparents and parents to share with children. Includes stories, poems, plays, proverbs and fables which will prompt discussion and help develop character and values.

Houtman, Sally. *To Grandma's House, We... Stay: When You Have to Stop Spoiling Your Grandchildren and Start Raising Them*. Studio 4 Productions, 1999. A road map for grandparents raising grandchildren that includes advice, information, and resources.

Kack-Brice, Valerie (ed). *For She is the Tree of Life: Grandmothers Through the Eyes of Women Writers.* Conari Press, 1995. A unique collection of heartwarming, evocative stories and photographs from female writers such as Marge Piercy, Maya Angelou, Margaret Atwood, and Leslie Marmon Silko.

Kettmann, Susan. *The 12 Rules of Grandparenting: A New Look at Traditional Roles and How to Break Them.* Facts on File, 2000. A practical book that helps grandparents create a role that works for them.

Kitzinger, Sheila. *Becoming a Grandmother: A Life Transition.* HarperCollins, 1996. A look at the passage into grandmotherhood, and finding satisfaction and enjoyment in relationships with adult children and grandchildren.

Kornhaber, Arthur. *The Grandparent Guide: The Definitive Guide to Coping with the Challenges of Modern Grandparenting.* McGraw-Hill, 2002. By a grandparenting pioneer, this comprehensive book addresses the diverse, complex role of being a grandparent today.

Kornhaber, Arthur. *The Grandparent Solution: How Parents Can Build a Family Team for Practical, Emotional, and Financial Success.* Jossey-Bass, 2004. Advice and tips for ensuring grandchildren have a close relationship with grandparents, and parents get the practical and emotional support they need to do the best job possible.

Marshall, Carl with David Marshall. *The Book of Myself: A Do-It-Yourself Autobiography in 201 Questions.* Hyperion, 1997. This grandfather/grandson team have created a keepsake "fill-in" book that's fun and has excellent memory prompts.

Martz, Sandra and Shirley Coe (eds). *Generation to Generation: Reflections on Friendships Between Young and Old*. Papier-Mache, 1998. An inspiring collection of stories, poems, photos.

Moore, Robin. *Creating a Family Storytelling Tradition*. August House, 1999. A great guide for creating, telling, and listening to stories.

Newman, Susan. *Little Things Mean A Lot: Creating Happy Memories with Your Grandchildren*. Crown, 1996. Hundreds of quick little ideas and inspirations to build close, meaningful relationships with your grandchildren.

Pipher, Mary. *The Shelter of Each Other: Rebuilding Our Families*. Ballantine, 1996. A practical, hopeful book about nurturing families.

Schaefer, Dan and Christine Lyons. *How Do We Tell the Children?: A Step-by-Step Guide for Helping Children Cope When Someone Dies* (third edition). Newmarket Press, 2001. An excellent book. Discusses age-appropriate messages and includes a quick-reference section.

Stone, Douglas and Bruce Patton, Sheila Heen. *Difficult Conversations: How to Discuss What Matters Most*. Viking, 1999. Based on the work of the Harvard Negotiation Project, this is a very useful, step-by-step guide for dealing with difficult situations of all types.

Trelease, Jim. *The Read-Aloud Handbook* (5th edition). Penguin, 2001. A classic! Read to grandchildren and encourage them to become avid readers themselves. Includes a treasury of read-aloud suggestions.

Wassermann, Selma. *The Long Distance Grandmother* (fourth edition). Hartley & Marks, 2001. A great source of practical, creative ideas for nurturing relationships with grandchildren who don't live nearby.

Westheimer, Ruth K. *Grandparenthood.* Routledge, 1998. Information and advice on grandparenting in Dr. Ruth's own inimitable style.

Zullo, Kathryn and Allan Zullo. *The Nanas and the Papas: A Boomer's Guide to Grandparenting.* Andrews McMeel, 1998. This modern guide includes defining your grandparenting role, dealing with adult children, and legal and financial issues.

---

www.2young2retire.com. A website filled with information, ideas, resources, and links for people over 50 who want to stay active and involved through new careers, hobbies, community/volunteer work, and more.

www.geezer.com. A source of unique, quality handcrafted gifts, apparel, and keepsakes made by older adult artisans. A project funded in part by the US Department of Labor and operated by Experience Works, a nonprofit organization. It provides senior artisans, crafters, and hobbyists across the country with the opportunity to supplement their income, launch new businesses, expand the market for their handcrafted goods, change negative stereotypes about aging, and improve their lives through meaningful activity. Browse all the wonderful handcrafted items (a great place to buy gifts for any occasion) or get information on becoming a Geezer.com artisan.

www.grandboomers.com. A website geared to baby boomer grandparents.

www.grandparents-day.com. Ideas for celebrating national Grandparents Day in September, including activities and contests.

www.legacyproject.org. The Legacy Project is a national community service initiative in partnership with the non-profit Parenting Coalition and Generations United in Washington, DC. Susan V. Bosak, author of *How to Build the Grandma Connection* and *Something to Remember Me By* is the Founding Chair. The project helps you build and maintain closer family bonds and celebrates the important legacies passed down from generation to generation. This award-winning website offers free online activity kits for family fun with grandchildren, guides, tip sheets, resource listings, books, contests, workshops, and more. For more information, you can also call (800) 772-7765.

www.myfamily.com. Provides a unique way to connect and strengthen families. In a secure, password-protected environment, MyFamily.com users can hold family discussions, create online family photo albums, maintain a calendar of family events, share family history information, and buy gifts for family members quickly and easily. The site also offers an easy-to-use template for a private family website. The site is part of MyFamily.com, Inc, the leading online network for connecting families with their histories and one another. The company also publishes *Ancestry Magazine*, *Genealogical Computing Magazine*, Ancestry Family Tree software, over 50 book titles, the 1-2-3 Family Tree package, and databases on CD-ROM.

Index

About the Author

Susan V. Bosak, MA, is an intergenerational researcher, educator, and bestselling author. She leads popular Grandma Connection Workshops and is also Chair of the national Legacy Project. She has degrees in Human Communication, English, and Sociology. She travels extensively doing workshops and keynote presentations, and is a popular radio and television guest. Articles on her work have appeared in publications across the country including *The Washington Post, Newsday, Chicago Sun-Times, Woman's Day, Parade, Reader's Digest New Choices,* and *Ageless Magazine.*

Susan is the author of several books. Her award-winning bestseller *Something to Remember Me By* inspired the Legacy Project. With richly-detailed, watercolor illustrations by artist Laurie McGaw, the 32-page picture book about love and legacies across generations tells the heartwarming story of the special relationship between a grandmother and granddaughter over the years. It's a popular gift book for grandchildren, mothers, and grandmothers.

Dream: A Tale of Wonder, Wisdom & Wishes is illustrated by fifteen of the top artists in the world. An inspiring celebration of hopes and dreams across a lifetime, it combines gorgeous illustrations with a beautifully told poetic story. It's a special gift grandparents can give a new grandchild, and a book they can share with older grandchildren to help them pursue their own dreams and goals.

Ask for *Something to Remember Me By* and *Dream* at your local bookstore, or visit www.legacyproject.org for more information.

Le?acy

PAST I PRESENT I FUTURE
WWW.LEGACYPROJECT.ORG

The Legacy Project offers grandparents and parents free online activity kits for family fun with children, guides, tip sheets, resource listings, books, contests, workshops, and more. It helps you build and maintain closer family bonds and celebrates the important legacies passed down from generation to generation. Visit the website at www.legacyproject.org or call 1-800-772-7765 for more information.